To Jill,

on the occasion of your 70th birthday,

Love from Elaine

LOST ELYSIUM?

LOST ELYSIUM?

*The Transformation of Middlesex
from Countryside to Suburbia as Seen
by Eye Witnesses*

Richard Piper

The Book Guild Ltd
Sussex, England

First published in Great Britain in 2005 by
The Book Guild Ltd
25 High Street
Lewes, East Sussex
BN7 2LU

Typesetting in Times by
Acorn Bookwork Ltd, Salisbury, Wiltshire

Printed in Great Britain by
CPI Bath

A catalogue record for this book is available from
The British Library.

ISBN 1 85776 889 2

MIDDLESEX

Gaily into Ruislip Gardens
Runs the red electric train,
With a thousand Ta's and Pardon's
Daintily alights Elaine;
Hurries down the concrete station
With a frown of concentration,
Out into the outskirt's edges
Where a few surviving hedges
Keep alive our lost Elysium – rural Middlesex again.

Well cut Windsmoor flapping lightly,
Jacqmar scarf of mauve and green
Hiding hair which, Friday nightly,
Delicately drowns in Drene;
Fair Elaine the bobby-soxer,
Fresh-complexioned with Innoxa,
Gains the garden – father's hobby –
Hangs her Windsmoor in the lobby,
Settles down to sandwich supper and the television screen.

Gentle Brent, I used to know you
Wandering Wembley-wards at will,
Now what change your waters show you
In the meadowlands you fill!
Recollect the elm-trees misty
And the footpaths climbing twisty
Under cedar-shaded palings,
Low laburnum-leaned-on railings,
Out of Northolt on and upward to the heights of Harrow Hill.

Parish of enormous hayfields
Perivale stood all alone,
And from Greenford scent of mayfields
Most enticingly was blown
Over market gardens tidy,
Taverns for the bona fide,
Cockney anglers, cockney shooters,
Murray Poshes, Lupin Pooters
Long in Kensal Green and Highgate silent under soot and stone.

Sir John Betjeman

Contents

Acknowledgements

Extracts from contemporary published accounts are an important element of this book and the original works are listed, with publishers and dates of publication, where known, in *Primary sources* at the end of the *Foreword*.

I would like to thank all those who helped me in the search for current owners of the copyrights and I can confidently say that every effort has been made to trace them. However, sometimes the trail met a dead end and I and the publishers would be pleased to hear from any copyright owners not acknowledged, in order to include their details in future editions.

Middlesex by Sir John Betjeman is reproduced by permission of John Murray Publishers.

Extracts from *The King's England – Middlesex* are used by permission of AM Heath Ltd.

Extracts from *Where to Live Round London – Northern Side* are used by permission of Frederick Warne & Co./Ladybird Books Ltd.

The Buildings of England – Middlesex has been succeeded by *The Buildings of England, London 3: North West* by Bridget Cherry and Nikolaus Pevsner and published by Yale University Press, whose permission for the quotations has been given.

Thanks are also due to The Orion Publishing Group Ltd. (Cassell) and to John Menzies PLC.

Two of the illustrations are reproduced by courtesy of London's Transport Museum and I would like to thank the team there, particularly David Bownes and Hugh Robertson, for their help.

The striking modern photographs were taken by my friend and former colleague Greg Ward, with whom I made several pleasant Metro-land forays. I also very much appreciate the work of Neil Douek in setting up the www.lostelysium.com website.

Last but not least I would like to thank my wife Heather not just for putting up with me (correct at time of writing) but also for continuing to earn an honest crust while I worked on the book, thus stopping me from starving in an author's garret.

Richard Piper

Foreword

I come from Sussex stock and am proud of it, now even in the cricket season. But I have lived most of my life in different parts of the county of Middlesex and it is also in my blood. This despite the fact that in the eyes of many it no longer exists [*except* as a cricket team]. Successive soulless, centralising, socialistic governments [national and local] have betrayed it and continue to keep it down, whilst their lackeys at the BBC as a matter of routine refer to [say] Harrow or Hillingdon as being in north west [sometimes west or north, they are not strong on geography] LONDON. To be fair, which I hate, it *looks* like part of London, with a ride on the Metropolitan line from Baker Street passing more or less continuous development as far as the county borders at Uxbridge or Northwood. But a hundred years ago it looked nothing like that. It was a county of fields, farms and tiny villages. It is difficult to imagine that anywhere in the country has changed as much in that time, and it is even more remarkable that much of this change took place in just twenty years between the end of one world war and the start of another.

Because the inhabitants of Middlesex are not [or at least not all] the rootless, grey suburbanites that they are sometimes painted, some of them have an interest in what things used to be like and how they came to be as they are now, and many books have been written in response. One such is the excellent *Eastcote – From Village to Suburb* by Ron Edwards. It is a good read, but I get a little concerned that such works in general, written with the benefit of hindsight, may present an over-rosy view of the past and too negative a one of the present.

Even the immortal Betjeman, whose poem *Middlesex* above

reflects my feelings in so many ways, may be at fault. Thinking back to his Edwardian childhood from the perspective of the early 1950s, he paints an idyllic picture of the "gentle Brent ... Wandering Wembley-wards at will", in sharp contrast with its subsequent murky, concrete-lined appearance near Hanger Lane. But J. Tavenor-Perry, writing about the Brent in *Memorials of Old Middlesex* published three years after Betjeman was born, refers to "all the impurities gathered on its way through Neasden ... and the poison in the waters with which it has become impregnated. Not so many years ago the river ... was full of fish ... but the chemical overflows have now made it a dead stream". A rather different image!

The theme of this book is to look at the development of a number of villages in north west Middlesex through contemporary eyes at different periods, followed by my own observation of those "villages" as they are today. At the core is a series of accounts from the books listed at the end of this Foreword. Their original publication dates range from 1876 to 1951 and they are written from a variety of perspectives, ranging from the most conservative of topographers to the enthusiastic promoters of building development. But they are all *contemporary*, recording how the places looked and how they were changing at the time for good or ill.

It is not my aim to supersede the accounts that have already given the background to, and details of, the process of suburbanisation. Indeed, in giving a brief summary of it I freely acknowledge my debt to two of them in particular: *London's Underground Suburbs* by Dennis Edwards and Roy Pigram, and *Semi-Detached London* by Alan A. Jackson. It seems, and perhaps this should not come as a surprise granted the scale of the changes, that there was no one single cause, but a raft of different ones all coming together.

First, the demand was there. The population of London was increasing, partly due to immigration linked to London's prosperity relative to the rest of the country, even [or perhaps especially] during the Depression. This prosperity was a consequence of continuing growth both in "new", clean consumer industries, such as electronics and consumer durables, and in services and administration. Improved education gave more young men the opportunity to take these white-collar jobs, with their higher pay and better security. Such people did not want to live in the cramped, dark, dirty, unhygienic conditions of central London and the older, Victorian suburbs. They wanted light and air, bathrooms and inside lavatories, labour-saving electric devices [which were unavailable to people in rented, gaslit accommodation], respectability and social status, and they looked for it *in the country*.

So what about the supply? Middlesex was there on the doorstep. Flat, open, sparsely populated and agriculturally depressed, as London's previously insatiable demand for hay declined and eventually disappeared. Immediately after World War I skilled labour was scarce, building materials were expensive and most of the new "homes fit for heroes" were provided by local authorities. However, during the course of the 1920s subsidies switched to private housing, the cost of building materials went down, interest rates declined and assistance with personal finance increased, and additional labour arrived from depressed areas. This was a glorious opportunity for the "speculative builder", a description that carries its negative baggage down the years, although it only means that they built houses without a specific buyer in mind and then had to sell them. In other words, what we would consider normal practice today.

The link between demand and supply was public transport, in particular the railways and "Underground" [mostly, of course, running over ground]. The growth of these in the second half of the 19th century and first half of the 20th was often followed by new residential development, though not necessarily immediately. Now indeed a man [of course] could work "in Town" and live "in the country", and the pre-

11

eminent railway company making it possible, certainly in the area under consideration, was the Metropolitan. Uniquely, the "Met" was directly involved in housing development itself, using land acquired before the railway was built. There are many books covering its growth and activities, some of which are listed below in *Further Reading*, but a concise overview can be found in Oliver Green's introduction to a reprint of the 1932 edition of *Metro-land*, published by Oldcastle Books in 1988. [He himself credits Alan Jackson's *London's Metropolitan Railway*, David and Charles 1986.] The involvement of the Met in housing development started in the 19th century but really went into full gear with the formation of a property company called Metropolitan Railway Country Estates Ltd in 1919, presaged by the first publication of *Metro-land* in 1915. *Metro-land* was a guide book full of "evocative descriptions and pictures of the historic villages and rural vistas" in what it called "London's nearest countryside", directed partly at hikers and day trippers but primarily at potential home owners, who represented "the means for building a captive market of season ticket holding passengers". But Metro-land was not just a guide book but a total, and brilliant, marketing concept. It had a physical location in north west Middlesex and parts of Herts and Bucks, but also one in the country of the mind. Green quotes from the 1920 edition: "The strain which the London business or professional man [!] has to undergo amidst the turmoil and bustle of Town can only be counteracted by the quiet restfulness and comfort of a residence amidst pure air and rural surroundings, and whilst jaded vitality and taxed nerves are the natural penalties of modern conditions, Nature has, in the delightful districts abounding in Metro-land, placed a potential remedy ready at hand." The prose, again as pointed out by Green, could be over the top in its attempt to blend age-old tradition with civilised progress: "This is a good parcel of English soil in which to build home and strike root, inhabited from of old ...

12

the new settlement of Metro-land proceeds apace; the new colonists thrive amain." But the message was strong, clear, and very successful. [In the text I have used italics to distinguish *Metro-land* the publication from Metro-land the place/concept. I have also retained the original hyphen, though some of the sources that I quote do not.]

The process was eventually stopped by a combination of Green Belt legislation and Adolf Hitler, but not before, according to Green, it had " ... transformed many districts from open countryside to drab and monotonous suburban sprawl. The notion of Metro-land as a rural Arcadia certainly no longer matched the suburban reality of Wembley Park or Rayners Lane, although the outer areas beyond Rickmansworth still retained their country character." There is clearly some truth in this view, as anyone who drives from Rayners Lane to Ruislip can observe, but is it the whole truth?

The exploration of that truth is one of the main purposes of this book. As already stated, it looks at six or so [depending on whether Harrow is counted as one or more] villages as they were before the main development started and as it gathered speed, through a variety of contemporary eyes, followed by my own observations of them as they are today, recorded on one or more walks round each. Have the promises of Metro-land and the "speculative builders" been entirely broken, or can the 21st-century Middle Saxon still enjoy some of the offered rural bliss?

The quotations have been selected and edited solely on the basis of relevance to the subject and not to grind any particular axe. Their contemporary nature gives them a particular value and can also be intriguing. For instance, I am captivated by the 1934 reference to the "community of sunbathers with advanced ideas" whose activities at the Welsh Harp reservoir had been causing "the authorities" ... "some perturbation". Does this mean that they were stripping to the buff or merely that sunbathing itself was an "advanced idea"? Any observa-

13

tions, corrections or additional insights that readers may have will be very welcome, and I would like to think of taking them into account in a future edition.

This book was put together for my own interest and, I hope, that of others. I try at the end to see whether the Middlesex experience has a broader relevance at a time when the current Government has ambitious plans to "concrete the countryside". But it is not a polemic, it is a labour of love.

Richard Piper
Ickenham, Middlesex

Primary sources

Initials in brackets are referenced in the text. Excerpts are set out in chronological order in each chapter, except that the three editions of *Metro-land* are taken together in order to highlight the pattern of development.

Pre 1914

Handbook to the Environs of London [HEL] James Thorne, 1876, 1970 reprint, Adams & Dart

Our Lanes and Meadowpaths [OLM] H. J. Foley, Truslove & Shirley, *c.* 1890

Greater London [GL] Edward Walford, Cassell & Co. Ltd, 1898

King's Directory [of Uxbridge] [KDU] 1903

Middlesex [MF] John B. Firth, Methuen & Co., 1906

Middlesex [MFH] John Fulleylove/A. R. Hope Moncrieff, A & C Black, 1907

Country Rambles Round Uxbridge [CRU] Stephen Springall, Lucy & Birch, Uxbridge, 1907

The Skirts of the Great City [SGC] Mrs Arthur G. Bell, Methuen & Co., 1907

Where To Live Round London – Northern Side [WTL] The Homeland Association Ltd/Frederick Warne & Co., 1908

Highways and Byways in Middlesex [HBI] Walter Jerrold, Macmillan & Co. Ltd, 1909

Memorials of Old Middlesex [MOM] J. Tavenor-Perry, Bemrose & Sons Ltd, 1909

1920–1951

Metro-land [ML] 1921, 1928, 1932 [last edition]. 1932 edition reprint, with Introduction by Oliver Green, Oldcastle Books/London Transport Museum, 1987

London and the British Empire Exhibition [LBE] Ward Lock & Co., 1924

Rural Nooks Round London [RNR] Charles G. Harper, Cecil Palmer, 1924

The Fringe of London [FOL] Gordon S. Maxwell, Cecil Palmer, 1925

Just Beyond London [JBL] Gordon S. Maxwell, Methuen & Co. Ltd, 1927

London and Suburbs Old and New [LAS] Frank Green and Dr Sidney Wolff, Souvenir Magazines Ltd, 1933

Middlesex Old and New [MON] Martin S. Briggs, George Allen & Unwin Ltd, 1934

London's Countryside [LC] Edric Holmes, Robert Scott, ?

The Face of London [TFL] Harold P. Clunn, Simpkin Marshall Ltd, 6th edition, 1935

15

The King's England – Middlesex [KEM] Ed. Arthur Mee, Hodder and Stoughton Ltd, 1940/1947

The Face of London and *The Face of the Home Counties* [FHC] Harold P. Clunn, Spring Books, "New" editions [no dates]

The Buildings of England, Middlesex [BEM] Nikolaus Pevsner, Penguin Books, 1951

Further reading

At the end of each chapter I have given a list of relevant further reading. This does not claim to be exhaustive but reflects the books that I have in my own collection. I have checked points in some of them in the process of preparing this book, but have tried to limit myself as far as possible to the contemporary sources and my own observations.

As far as this Foreword is concerned, several key sources have already been acknowledged, and these works are listed below, along with others of relevance to the growth of the London suburbs in general and those of Middlesex in particular. They are listed in the order of their original publication.

Middlesex, The Jubilee of the County Council 1889–1939 C.W. Radcliffe, Evans Brothers, 1939

The County Books Series, Middlesex Norman G. Brett-James, Robert Hale Limited, 1951

The Metropolitan Railway C. Baker, The Oakwood Press, 1951

Middlesex Michael Robbins, Collins, 1953 [Reprinted Phillimore, 2003]

A History of the County of Middlesex [The Victoria History of the Counties of England.] *Volume 3* Susan Reynolds [ed.], University of London, 1984 [1962]

16

A History of the County of Middlesex [The Victoria History of the Counties of England.] *Volume 4* J.S. Cockburn and T.F.T. Baker [eds.], Oxford University Press, 1971

Middlesex Bruce Stevenson, B.T. Batsford Ltd, 1972

Semi-Detached London Alan A. Jackson, Wild Swan Publications Ltd, 1991 [1973]

Metro Memories Dennis Edwards and Ron Pigram, Bloomsbury Books, 1988 [1977]

What's In A Name? Cyril M. Harris, Archway Publishing, 3rd edition, 1990 [1977]

John Betjeman's Collected Poems John Murray, 1979

The Romance of Metro-land Dennis Edwards and Ron Pigram, Bloomsbury Books, 1988 [1979]

A Guide to the Architecture of London Edward Jones & Christopher Woodward, Phoenix Illustrated, 1997 [1983/1992]

Betjeman Country Frank Delaney, Hodder and Stoughton/ John Murray, 1983

The Golden Years of the Metropolitan Railway Dennis Edwards and Ron Pigram, Bloomsbury Books, 1988 [1983]

The London Encyclopaedia Ben Weinreb and Christopher Hibbert [eds], Macmillan, 1983

England in Cameracolour, Middlesex John Bethell and Philip Scoones, Town & County Books Ltd, 1984

The Art and Architecture of London Ann Saunders, Phaidon, 1988 [1984]

The Making of Modern London, 1914–1939 Gavin Weightman and Steve Humphries, Sidgwick and Jackson, 1984

London's Underground Suburbs Dennis Edwards and Ron Pigram, Bloomsbury Books, 1988 [1986]

The Village London Atlas The Village Press, 1989 [1986]

Metro-land 1932 Edition Oliver Green [intro.], Oldcastle Books/London Transport Museum, 1987

The Middlesex Village Book Middlesex Federation of Women's Institutes/Countryside Books, 1989

The Buildings of England, London 3: North West Bridget Cherry and Nikolaus Pevsner, Penguin Books, 1991

The Times London History Atlas Hugh Clout [ed.], Times Books, 1991

Middlesex Within Living Memory Middlesex Federation of Women's Institutes/Countryside Books, 1996

The Piccadilly Line Desmond F. Croome, Capital Transport, 1998

London Suburbs Merrell Holberton/English Heritage, 1999

London A Historical Companion Kenneth Panton, Tempus, 2003 [2001]

1

"Wonderful Wembley"

I start my search in Wembley; the beginning of Metro-land and the place where I spent the first ten years of my life. As a small child it never occurred to me that it had ever had any connection with the countryside, or that it was only twenty years since Keswick Gardens, the unpretentious cul-de-sac where we lived, had been "planned and developed along the best Garden Suburb lines" by Comben and Wakeling. Years later, however, in a pub in Oxford an old boy told me that in his youth he often visited Wembley to see his brother, who was a shepherd, and a vision of Wembley and Middlesex more generally as rural areas started to open out.

In 1876 James Thorne refers to it as merely

... a hamlet of Harrow-upon-the Hill ...

and mentions

... the Rev. John Edw. Gray, whose seat, Wembley Park, is the manor house. The park extends E. of the hamlet towards Kingsbury, is large, varied in surface, abundantly timbered, and watered by a branch of the Brent.

Very salubrious it is too.

Wembley Hill is celebrated for the prospects from the summit, though the distant country westward is cut off by the heights of Harrow. The Green Man, with its gardens, on the top of the hill is much frequented by holiday parties and for trade dinners. The walks by the lanes from Wembley Park to Kingsbury, the Hyde, and Hendon or Whitchurch, are very pleasant.

But change is in the air:

About the church has grown up a little colony of villas and cottages, with a cottage-hospital, a district school, a working men's hall, and a young men's institute. [HEL]

A few years later Foley says,

... we wend our way up Wembley Hill. A curious out-of-the-way hamlet it is, half buried in its own trees, and one might pass through it and very likely not see the greater number of cottages of which it is composed.

... we come to the gates of Wembley Park, with an ivy-grown and thatch-covered lodge guarding the entrance ... some 250 acres, beautifully wooded, chiefly on high ground, but undulating to a branch of the River Brent which runs through it.

... we may, by a charming lane from the lodge gates, continue to skirt Wembley Park for upwards of a mile. After leaving the lodge we pass a very pretty three-gabled cottage, set deep in a rich garden.... .

Though not far from this idyll lurks

...the straggling and unattractive hamlet of Alperton. [OLM]

With Walford [1898] we return to Arcadia:

Here, in the neighbourhood of Harrow and Kingsbury, the fields are still green, the hedgerows fresh, the forest trees put on their summer garb as of yore, and even the smaller streams,

20

which here and there expand into broad lakes and ponds, are not yet forced to burrow underground.

With the exception, perhaps, of Vienna, there is no capital in Europe with scenery so beautiful, and so easily accessible.

A strong claim, indeed, but the forces of change are on the move:

The manor has been acquired by the Metropolitan Railway Company, who have sold and leased portions of it to the Metropolitan Tower Construction Company Limited, for the purposes of a holiday resort. . . .

. . . cricket and football grounds, and a running track which is one of the largest in England; there is a lake eight acres in extent, spanned by ornamental bridges; there are pavilions, tea pagodas, bandstands, lawns and terraces. And as the centre of all these attractions is to be . . . the Watkin Tower . . . . When completed, it will be able to boast a stature of 1,200 feet. It will thus be taller by 200 feet than the Eiffel Tower . . . . *[GL]*

Three years later Firth is a little less positive:

The [manor] house, a large, pleasantly situated building, is now fast falling into utter ruin. The Wembley Park Estate was bought by the Metropolitan Railway Company, who carried their line through it and sold and leased portions of it to a company, which laid out large sums in converting the park into a spacious pleasure ground. The attractions include a partly completed tower, called the Watkin Tower . . . .It has . . . not got beyond the first stage, and will evidently rise no higher.

. . . Wembley Park, that ambitious attempt at a north-western pleasure palace, whose stumpy Tower of Babel, long at a stick, will now cease to be a landmark and an eyesore. *[MF]*

21

By 1908 Wembley is not just for local yokels or hordes of trippers, and *Where to Live Round London* is singing its praises:

> ... situated amid pleasant rural surroundings ... Wembley is well circumstanced for residential purposes. The older portion of the village stands around the parish church of St John, but the main business street extends for some distance along the Harrow road, residential thoroughfares spreading out on either side.

> The district is growing rapidly. Its most picturesque part lies adjacent to the well-known Wembley Park, a finely timbered expanse of some 280 acres, originally intended to serve as one of London's playgrounds .... Preparations are being made for laying it out for villa residences of a substantial character.

> The air is bracing and the whole neighbourhood healthy, with a good water supply. There are many villa residences of a pleasing character letting at moderate rents.

Note the reference to letting rather than the property-owning democracy to come! However the advertisement for George H. Ward, builder at 1 The Parade, pinpoints the three key elements of Wembley's attraction:

> Health, beautiful country, splendid train services. *[WTL]*

A year later Jerrold still highlights the pastoral:

> And indeed there is not much open country left now between the Metropolis and Harrow, though there are yet tree-grown fields about the lane towards Wembley, and between Wembley and Harrow, and some rural bits along the Brent valley. Wembley Park itself is a beautiful extent of between two and three hundred acres of well-timbered ground, overlooking the

Brent valley towards Willesden. *[HBI]*

By 1921, the land is returning to peace, the heroes are looking for homes, Metro-land the dream has been born and *Metro-land* the publication is selling Wembley hard, albeit with a degree of honesty about its rural nature.

The dweller at Wembley Park can be swept from the depths of the City into rural, or at all events, semi-rural country .... That is what living at Wembley Park means to the London business man.

Wembley Park is not, like so many urban "Parks" a park merely in name. It looks like a park, possesses all the properties of a park, and is, in fact, a park, providing every essential to qualify it for that designation. There are picturesque scenery, beautiful trees, a lovely, green, undulating landscape, and some artistic dwelling houses, not a great many as yet, but sufficient to show an example for more.

There are two important building estates at Wembley Park, the Wembley Park Estate, with 280 acres, and the Chalk Hill Estate, with 123. Both are in process of development. On the Chalk Hill Estate it is intended to erect over a hundred small houses on plots of half an acre or upwards, which can be acquired on the gradual purchase system.

The advertisement for the estates makes strong claims about their rural location.

... within close touch of London, yet in the open country beyond the recognised suburban area.

This estate comprises over 120 acres of very fine undulating Land, with ideal surroundings ....

The supporting text says

23

The Chalk Hill Estate ... has been planned out in half-acre and acre plots for the erection of small houses of a country type, with ample grounds for gardens and orchards. *[ML 1921]*

A rural dream indeed, but seven years later the tone is very different:

The British Empire Exhibition, which made the name of Wembley famous throughout the World in 1924 and 1925, is now only a memory. But the site and some of its more important buildings are being used for a variety of industrial purposes connected with motors, films, etc.

Wembley Park itself has now settled down to the every-day activities of a residential suburb, and thanks to the enterprising activities of several Estate Companies, on both sides of the railway, is already a popular township which is rapidly going ahead.

And a new estate is coming into being:

... Haymills Ltd. is dealing with a fine triangular site, approximately 196 acres in extent on the southern and eastern slopes of Barn Hill. This, until two years ago, was entirely undeveloped. The company has already put up a large number of well-built houses of various types and a few years will undoubtedly suffice to see the completion of this Estate as one of the most attractive and desirable suburbs of London. Some forty acres on the upper part of Barn Hill have been acquired by the Wembley council for a public park for the benefit of local residents.

One thing that has not changed is the ad for the Chalk Hill and Wembley Park Estates, which are still "in the open country beyond the recognised suburban area"! And to give me somewhere to live twenty years later:

24

Prince's Court, Sudbury Court and St. Augustine's Estates ...
are planned and developed on the best Garden Suburb lines –
with semi-detached houses to suit all tastes and requirements.
£750 to £1250
Comben and Wakeling Ltd.

Nice houses, but NOT in the same league as the Barn Hill
Estate:

280 feet above sea level
Situated on the Southern and Western slopes of Barn Hill in
the health-giving air of the open country ...
Prices £1175 to £2000
Haymills Houses *[ML 1928]*

In 1932 progress continues, though not everything in the
garden city is lovely:

Many of the Exhibition buildings are being used for a variety
of industrial purposes, but the final clearing up of this large site
is still a long way from completion.

As a residential suburb Wembley Park is developing rapidly.
Over five thousand houses have been built within the past few
years and there is no sign of abatement in the demand. A particularly pleasant colony has arisen on the slopes of Wembley
Hill, and on the north side of the line the old Kingsbury Road
has become a flourishing "Main Street".

Hundreds of houses being built in the neighbourhood including
the Chalk Hill, Barn Hill, Townsend Park, South Forty Lane
and Kingsbury Park, etc., Estates. *[ML 1932]*

But in the ad the Chalk Hill Estate is *still* "in the open
country beyond the recognised suburban area"!
To catch up on the Stadium and the Exhibition, we can go

back a few years to the Ward Lock Red Guide for 1924:

> During the summer of 1923 work *[on the Exhibition]* began in
> real earnest. Bit by bit the rural character of Wembley Park
> was transformed by forests of iron and steel rods sprouting
> from boxes which moulded the concrete poured in from giant
> elevators.
>
> Among other alterations may be noted the filling-in of a large
> lake on the site now occupied by the North Entrance. Of his-
> torical interest was the demolition of the foundations of the
> former Wembley Tower, begun in 1880 in imitation of the
> Eiffel Tower, but never carried beyond the first stage. The site
> is now occupied by the Stadium. *[LBE]*

Amidst this progress Gordon S. Maxwell [1925] is still seeking
rural Wembley:

> The sight I mean was the old-world bits of the village, which
> despite its rapid "modernization", are still to be found, and the
> many little farms – some still delightfully rural – that lie on its
> outskirts.
>
> The lodge of the old Wembley Park is still there today, a little
> one-storied brick building; it is so swamped, however, by its
> giant neighbours, that it is never noticed. ... This lodge and
> mutilated drive are all that is left of this fine old estate as it was
> in the days when the British Empire itself, let alone the Exhibi-
> tion, was undreamed of.

And he does not seem to have bought into the Metro-land
garden city/village concept!

> A guide book informs us that "the development of Wembley
> Park as a garden city was arrested by the War". It is sometimes
> a pity they don't arrest a few more! ... the idea is a good one

... but it seems inevitable that garden cities attract cranks as surely as rotten apples attract wasps. Most of these places belie their name by not having the least resemblance to gardens and being quite unlike cities .... .

Perhaps Maxwell is being misled here by a name into believing that there were plans for development of a real garden city, like Letchworth. Such places do appear to have had a reputation for attracting "cranks", as exemplified by "Biggleswick" in John Buchan's *Mr Standfast*, but the use of the term in a Metro-land context seems rather to have been a sexed-up way of describing an estate of houses with gardens. In any case, Maxwell is more interested in the old Wembley than the new.

... my starting point was Oakington Farm, which lies on the high ground at the back of the Stadium. Though the surroundings of the farm have now lost nearly all of their rural look, it still bears traces of its former unspoiled days, notably the fine old farm-yard, with its quaint water trough, that lies directly behind the house.

In fact Maxwell's English rural idyll was enlivened by the sight of elephants, camels, llamas and "turbaned Hindoos", which were taking part in the Pageant of Empire! Moving on:

... I went along the road to Sudbury, entering Wembley Church on the way. Quite a modern structure, it is, however, a picturesque little building embowered amidst trees. To the right as he walks the rambler can see the wooded slopes of Horsendon [*sic*] Hill .... .

Vale Farm, standing back from the road up a small drive, has some picturesque buildings, but the place is quite spoiled now by the ultra-modern row of villas built in front of them. The gem of the district, however, is to be found at the neighbouring

Hundred Elms Farm, where just inside the farm-yard gate is probably the oldest and most picturesque building for many a mile. This is a well-preserved section of a monastic building, now descended to secular uses as a stable and granary.

There is a fine walk across the fields here to Preston, a small hamlet that skirts Wembley on the north. It is a walk as rural as the heart could wish, and for loneliness might be two hundred miles from London. ... The chief house is Uxendon Farm, which lies in the dip of the hill on which stand the "lattice-work" shooting-towers so conspicuous from the Stadium Terrace. This farm is by far the best of all round here for picturesque setting. It stands well back from the road down a long drive, and is almost hidden in a wooded valley through which runs a pleasant little stream. It is this stream – a tributary of the River Brent – that runs through the Exhibition grounds. ... I spent some time at Uxendon Farm, talking to the farmer and wandering round the old farm-yard buildings and fields. ... Almost within a stone's throw [by catapult] is the great Exhibition and a couple of hundred yards from the drive gates a "Met" station, yet the place had a peaceful old-world atmosphere about it that made me loath to go.

Maxwell points out that it was here that Anthony Babington and his followers were discovered and later executed for a plot to assassinate the first Queen Elizabeth and put Mary Queen of Scots on the throne and restore Roman Catholicism in England.

As I walked back to Wembley I was forcibly struck by how easily so big a place as the Exhibition can be lost sight of; it was not until I climbed the hill, on top of which stands the Green Man Inn, that I saw any signs of it at all.

The original Green Man was burned down some years since; it was a noted pleasure resort for Londoners as long ago as the

28

eighteenth century, when the place had extensive tea gardens, traces of which, decayed and desolate, can still be seen.

All told, however, his visit to the Wembley of 1924 has given him

... many unforgettable glimpses of that old England from which sprang the greatest Empire in the world. *[FOL]*

With *London and Suburbs Old and New* in 1933 we return to the estate agent style of describing the changing scene, and the action is moving further from central Wembley.

Of all the suburbs on the fringe of Outer London there are few, if any, that can compare with the semi-rural suburb of Sudbury and Sudbury Hill. ... Sudbury is surrounded by open country
. . . .

[*Preston*] This delightful spot ... situated in the midst of charming countryside and land of undulating character, can claim to be "unique", not only on account of its beautiful surroundings and salubrity, but from the fact that there is none of the deadly monotony which is sometimes to be found in newly developed districts .... A dominating feature of the landscape is Barn Hill – a public park – with its green slopes and tree-clad summit. ... the building process is sound and steady, rather than spectacular and rapid.

The advertisement of Mills and Co., Kinch Grove Estate, Preston Road waxes lyrical:

In the best part of Preston ... facing Lyon Farm. Carefully planned and soundly constructed houses of artistic merit and varied design, in an orchard setting of particular charm .... Most houses have open ground behind where building is prohibited or restricted.

[*Kingsbury*] There have been striking changes in the district of Kingsbury during the last ten years. ... population ... in 1921 ... was 1,855, whereas in 1932 it is approximately 20,000! ... It has a delightful situation, being just off the beaten track. It still retains much of its rural charm, and many open spaces have been preserved ... and there is charming surrounding country within easy walking distance or can be reached by bus. *[LAS]*

The last phrase is perhaps telling about the real situation as one could argue that the countryside is accessible by bus from Oxford Circus! A more objective view, uninfluenced by advertisers, can be obtained from Martin S. Briggs a year later.

The highest point is Barn Hill [282 feet], a beech-crowned knoll which forms a prominent landmark for miles around and has recently been acquired as public open space. Kingsbury Hill is now covered with houses, as is Wembley Hill [234 feet].

The Kingsbury authorities have had the foresight to purchase the fields bordering on the *[Welsh Harp]* lake as public open space, where a community of sunbathers with advanced ideas has recently caused them some perturbation. *[!]*

In 1922 began a great road-widening campaign in view of the coming exhibition, and several winding little lanes lost all their trees in the conversion into "Class A" motor highways. This was, in fact, the beginning of the end for Wembley of the old rural days.

... in the decennium 1921–31, Wembley's population had trebled [*to 48,546*] and that of Kingsbury had multiplied nine times. ... And this astounding increase seems to be continuing with unabated vigour throughout the district. In Kingsbury you are greeted with the slogan: "Eyes left for houses of Artistry", and, after all, who can resist that appeal? Certainly not John Citizen or his wife.

30

The farms which once were sparsely scattered over the district are rapidly disappearing: few of them had artistic merit of the first order, but nearly every one of them formed a charming group with great barns, their roofs tiled and their sides boarded. At the time of writing, a few still remain in Salmon Street, but their days are numbered. Oakington Manor Farm, near the Brent and close to the Stadium, has a long history rather than an architectural interest. Its fields are now nearly covered with the advancing sea of villas, and within a year or two at most it will be engulfed.

As for Wembley Park, that now devastated and depressing area ...

Of all its *[Empire Exhibition]* memories, only the massive stadium remains intact. ... In more senses than one, Wembley has gone to the dogs. The vast Exhibition site has been farmed out to a host of small industrial firms, who carry out their various enterprises amid the tawdry ruins of Burmese palaces and African fortresses. ... *Sic transit gloria mundi!* *[MON]*

This realism is also reflected by Harold P. Clunn in the 6th edition of *The Face of London* [1935], who does however have sad tidings of the Welsh Harp sunbathers with "advanced ideas":

The new craze for sunbathing has been freely indulged on the shores of the Welsh Harp lake, but on account of the objections raised by local inhabitants the apostles of this new pastime have been compelled to seek accommodation elsewhere. On the south side of the lake now runs the North Circular Road connecting Finchley with Wembley.

... the main street extends for some distance along the Harrow Road, where much building is still taking place.

Of late years Wembley [*Stadium area*] has become an industrial

31

centre and some of the exhibition buildings have been converted into factories.

... many new factories have been erected at Wembley ...

The post-war edition of *The Face of London* completes the
"countryside to suburb" story.

The old village of Wembley ... stood around the parish church
of St John-the-Evangelist, but all traces of it have vanished in
the rapid development of this flourishing suburb. ... In Harrow
Road, or Wembley High Road, which is the central shopping
area, are many attractive new terraces of shops extending
towards Sudbury Hill. There is an Odeon Cinema in Harrow
Road and a large Regal Cinema in Ealing Road. ... In 1938
the new Wembley Town Hall was erected on the north side of
Forty Lane .... It is said to have cost the Wembley ratepayers
a lot of money, but whatever its internal appointments, it more
closely resembles a factory or a large packing case than a ...
public building when viewed from outside. Carmel Court, next
to the Town Hall, is a new colony of flats for ladies only. Some
of the finest homes in Wembley are located in Park Lane,
Wembley Park Drive and on the high ground above Forty
Lane. King Edward VII Park which slopes down the hill on the
west side of Park Lane is a pleasant spot with panoramic views
of Harrow-on-the-Hill and the undulating country round Stanmore.

Raglan Gardens on the west side of Wembley Park, now
renamed Empire Way, is lined with new blocks of flats. Half a
mile north of Wembley Park Station is Barn Hill Recreation
Ground. This is Wembley's beauty spot and covers the top of a
steep hill from which fine views are obtained of Harrow-on-the-
Hill and the surrounding countryside.

Kingsbury, formerly a rural parish on the west side of the
Edgware Road, has of late years become a large industrial

32

suburb which was added to Wembley in 1934. The rapid growth of Kingsbury and the adjoining suburb of Queensbury has been furthered by the extension in 1933 of the Metropolitan Railway from Wembley Park to Stanmore .... Queensbury has an attractive shopping centre which is built round a turfed square and there is a larger one at Queensbury Circus in Honeypot Lane. *[TFL]*

So it is not just Wembley itself. Kingsbury is now a "large industrial suburb", and a similar picture is presented in *The King's England* [1940]:

To remember it had 5000 people when our century began and now has nearly 120,000 is to have some idea of the rapid growth of this place. ...

It has joined up with Kingsbury and Sudbury, forming one town for municipal purposes, and thousands of new houses, blocks of flats with beautiful gardens, new roads bordered with mown grass, and a 26-acre park are part of its picture. But the picture that comes to mind at the mention of Wembley is of its spectacular landmarks, the Stadium, the Municipal Buildings and the Electricity Station with its huge chimneys and enormous concrete water condenser.

Most of the permanent buildings of the Exhibition remain as factories, and the Stadium still stands on the hill, with flags flying from its twin towers.

At Sudbury is one of the finest open-air swimming baths in England. Of its old days there are, at Hundred Elms Farm, a brick outbuilding of the 16th century and a timbered barn of the 17th. *[KEM]*

Nikolaus Pevsner is not impressed with Wembley, albeit he is rather more positive than Clunn about the town hall:

33

There is uncommonly little of historic interest in this large borough [population in 1949, 132,000].

TOWN HALL, 1935–40, by Clifford Strange, the best of the modern town halls around London, neither fanciful nor drab. *[BEM]*

So, in the space of 75 years or fewer Wembley developed from a "little colony of villas and cottages" to a "flourishing suburb" or even a "town" of 130,000 people. But how did it feel as a place to live to people who had been promised "beautiful country" [1908] or houses "in the open country beyond the recognised suburban area" [Metro-land period]? Did it even feel like the "garden city" so disliked by Maxwell? How does the closest part of Metro-land to London strike the resident or visitor in the early years of the 21st century? To find out, I re-visit my childhood haunts on a bright and breezy day in mid March.

I start at my alma mater: Park Lane School. When school league tables were first published I checked it out and noted that it was the second worst school in the Borough of Brent, surely a hard accolade to win, but it has a history and pre-dates Metro-land. According to Geoffrey Hewlett: "It was the first council school to be built in Wembley and also preceded King Edward VII Park which was then sloping meadows where cattle grazed and haymakers worked in the summer. In its early days, children ... would be taken by the Misses Fowler and Birch to the banks of the river Brent for some of their lessons." Now my first teacher in the Infants was called Miss Birch, who was soon to retire and was surely the same lady, giving me a link to Wembley's past and indicating a remarkable lack of staff turnover in the Park Lane School of the first half of the 20th century. At first sight now there does not seem to be much sign of life, but returning at break time I can hear the happy noise across the park. No change there

34

then, but some things are different. The children look smart in red sweatshirts and black trousers, a nice change from our post-war hand-me-downs, and they appear to represent every ethnic group under the sun, whereas we were all the same colour and creed, leavened [if that's the right word] only by the Jewish kids. So the Wembley citizens of 2003 look very different from those of fifty years ago, but what if anything links them to the rural past?

Looking over the park, it seems much smaller than it used to [of course] but also more open, with views to the greenery of Harrow Hill and Weald that I don't remember being there, and this airy feeling persists as I drive along Park Lane. I can see the Barn Hill Estate ahead, looking attractive and with its houses well spaced, but my immediate goal is to see what is left of Wembley Park.

The first pleasant discovery is that the "ivy-grown and thatch-covered" lodge is still there, well maintained and with a modern extension. However, there is no park and the cottage is hemmed in by houses and the noisy road. Not much sign either of the "villa residences of a substantial character" envisaged in 1908. It is not even easy to envisage how the houses looked when they were built, owing to a proliferation of "improvements", such as stone cladding and extensions, and an absence of original windows and doors. There is no feeling of the country here now. It feels very enclosed.

Next I take a look at Tokyngton. No sign of the Oakington Farm house now, let alone the farm, just a rather bare patch of grass called Sherrins Farm Open Space, named it would appear from Hewlett after the last tenant E.H. Sherren [with an "e"] and currently with a view of the cranes towering over the ruins of the Stadium. The houses here are quintessential Wembley and none the worse for it: Tudorbethan semis, some quite substantial, all rather pleasant. I must have a suburban soul! The parish church of St Michael is rather nice in a plain sort of way. I note that the vicar styles himself "Father" and celebrates a Parish Mass, and that the little road alongside is called Babington Rise, so perhaps the Catholic cause Babington died for lives on, under the auspices of the Church of England. Viewed from here Wembley Hill looks very drab and urban, with barely a tree to be seen.

Now for the Prince's Court Estate and my old house. The sun comes out as I sit in my car opposite 8 Keswick Gardens. No front garden or privet hedge now, just a bricked drive with two cars on it, avoiding the difficulty of parking in the narrow road. There were fewer cars in the 1950s [we didn't have one ourselves until I was seven or eight] and presumably fewer still in 1927 when the houses were built. I look up the road towards what was my friend Peter Walker's house and it all still looks very nice, perhaps justifying the builder's claim that "These estates are planned and developed on the best Garden Suburb lines – with semi-detached houses to suit all tastes and requirements ... £750 to £1,250". I think that ours must have been a £750 one, though a look at the *Wembley Observer* indicates that in March 2003 it must be worth over £300,000. It backs on to the park and I see even now how the original residents, perhaps moving out of cramped accommodation in inner London, could have felt that they were moving into "rural, or at all events, semi-rural country", even though that is not how I saw it as a child. As I turn into Castleton Avenue I spot a Kosher deli van and am somehow reassured that the Jewish community is still here.

I have a quick lunch at the Green Man, which is pretty empty when I arrive, but soon heaving with some sort of office outing and therefore continuing to fulfil one of its functions of the last 130 years at the least. The views now are largely of bricks and mortar, but many of the houses are painted white, giving them an almost Mediterranean feel in the sunshine.

On to the Barn Hill Estate, the jewel in Wembley's crown, built by Haymills and sold at prices that started where the

Prince's Court Estate's stopped. The houses are big, both detached and semi-detached, and immaculately maintained. The preserved open space at the top means that this is one part of Wembley that really does feel as if it is in the countryside, or at least a piece of countryside in Wembley. This is where I used to come as a boy after we got a car [blue Ford Popular] on little outings to catch sticklebacks. The pond today looks reasonably free of litter, with reeds round the side and frogs mating. What better to do on a sunny spring day! The feeling you get here depends where you look. If you are outside the wood looking in, you are in the country. Looking out you can see the BT Tower, the Stock Exchange and Canary Wharf. The "dweller" really can be "swept from the depths of the City into ... [the] ... country".

My final stop is at Uxendon Crescent, where in 1924 Maxwell talked to the farmer and found "... a peaceful old world atmosphere ... that made me loath to go". It is a pleasant little road, very 1930s, but with no sign at all that the farm it is built on was once "by far the best of all round here for picturesque setting".

So does 21st-century Wembley live up to the *Metro-land* promises? Not entirely, but it never did. This is not only due to the inherent contradiction of Metro-land [if you build too many houses in the countryside it ceases to be the countryside] but also because Wembley [the "little colony of villas and cottages" near St John's church] was already there and now looks very run down, with the "flourishing Main Street" a scruffy disgrace that should be razed to the ground. As for Metro-land Wembley, its delivery on promises is patchy, seeming to come down to two, partly connected, issues: the amount and nature of the preserved open space and the price of the houses.

Further reading

Wembley Through The Ages Rev. H.W.R. Elsley, Wembley News, 1953

A History of Wembley Geoffrey Hewlett [ed.], Brent Library Service, 1979

Brent: A Pictorial History Len Snow, Phillimore, 1990

Britain in Old Photographs, Wembley & Kingsbury Adam Spencer, Alan Sutton Publishing, 1995

Images of London, Wembley Geoffrey Hewlett, Tempus, 2002

2

Ickenham: the last but one remaining village?

It must be a very long time since anyone living in Wembley thought of himself as living in a village. In Ickenham things are different. It is mostly bounded by open fields, with only a small connection with Ruislip at West Ruislip Station, and it is in many ways self-contained, with two churches, four schools, four pubs, a village hall and a residents' association ["the other IRA"]. There is farmland at the front of my house and from the study at the back as I write I can see across to Harrow Hill over luxuriant greenery. People here still refer to it as a village. But it has some 12,000 inhabitants, so in tracing its development and describing its current appearance I will try to examine the extent to which promises of homes in the country were met here and what, if anything, makes it different from another suburb.

When Thorne wrote in 1876 it certainly was

> ... an old fashioned country village, with the houses straggling along the lanes, and nestling a little more closely about the village green.

There was [and is] a

> ... village pump ... the very place for a little cosy village chat and scandal on an idle summer afternoon, – and beyond, on the farther side of the green, half hidden behind the tall trees, is

the village church: making altogether a very pretty village landscape.

It has to be said that it would be a rather noisy spot now for
"a little cosy village chat"!
   Ickenham also had [and has] its own stately home:

   ... the capital 17th century mansion of Swakeley,

amidst beautiful surroundings,

   ... and all around are broad green meadows, spotted here and
   there with farm houses that look the very picture of comfort
   and prosperity. *[HEL]*

Foley describes it in much the same way:

   ... another sequestered village, with its cottages planted around
   a central green. A tiny white church, with wooden belfry and
   dwarf spire, stands amid trees at a road corner on the right. ...
   The same wooden memorials of departed rustics adorn its
   churchyard, where the sheep are busy nibbling among the
   ancient graves.

   ... the broad park of Swakeleys. There is a public footpath
   right through it to Uxbridge Common ... *[OLM]*

Walford provides some additional details, including the
population size:

   ... the houses of which place, few in number, are located round
   the village green or scattered about in picturesque confusion in
   the surrounding lanes.

   ... the population in 1891 numbered only 396 souls, being an
   increase of 20 upon the census returns in 1881.

In the churchyard there is a very fine yew tree and at the west end of the church is an unsightly charnel-house belonging to the owner of Swakeleys.

He also describes the surroundings of Swakeleys:

... Swakeleys ... standing in an extensive park ... surrounded on all sides by broad green meadows and pasture-lands.

The grounds ... are somewhat flat, but well wooded, and are intersected by a little rivulet, which is dammed up into a miniature lake. The estate is strictly preserved, and the rabbits and pheasants walk and run about almost tame by the wayside ....

In nine years in Ickenham I have seen a large variety of wildlife, particularly birds, but never a pheasant. Until fairly recently, the closest rabbit that I had seen was at Harefield [!] though I now see that they disport themselves at the golf course at Harefield Place, which *is* in Ickenham. How long before they venture across the fields *Watership Down* style and invade my apology for a garden?

The gardens are quaint and trim ... and a long avenue of elms adorns the front of the house to the south. [*GL*]

King's Directory of Uxbridge for 1903 gives a similar estimate of the population [374] but only lists around 30 addresses. The occupations 100 years ago reflect the local economy and include bricklayer, keeper, hay dealer and wood dealer.

   With Firth we are back to Arcadian description:

Three-quarters of a mile to the SW of Ickenham village, and approachable thence by a pleasant footpath, is the fine Jacobean mansion of Swakeleys.

The grounds are charmingly wooded, and the river Pinn, which

41

flows through them, has been compelled, with much ingenuity, to serve the purpose of a long lake, in which are set little islands, well planted with trees, a paradise for wildfowl. The avenue, along which the path runs, forms a delightful retreat.

Uxbridge may be reached from Swakeleys by a pleasant footpath, which leads on to Uxbridge Common. *[MF]*

Just a year later, however, in 1907, Hope Moncrieff is describing some changes, though his emphasis remains on the pastoral:

... beyond the Great Western Railway station for both [*i.e., with Ruislip*] villages, each of them having an adjacent "halt" of the Metropolitan line, that begins to sow villas on the fields it has ploughed up, where as yet real cottages bear their crop of ruddy cheeks and hobnailed boots. Ickenham seems still a quieter and quainter hamlet than Ruislip; ...

This, like a true country village, lies under the squirely shadow of Swakeleys, the best preserved seventeenth-century manor-hall left in Middlesex, if Holland House be put out of account. *[MFH]*

Jerrold in 1909 also mentions development, advancing from the direction of big brother Ruislip.

North of Ickenham lies a larger old village, that of Ruislip – with building going on in the immediate neighbourhood, and threatening before many years are past to link the two villages, since the railway came hither. [*HBI*]

World War I brought further substantial change, as described by *Metro-land* in 1921:

The little village preserves its staid and venerable appearance;

42

but in the course of the war an enormous aircraft works made its appearance in the vicinity, and with the influx of alien influences the drowsy atmosphere of Ickenham village is rapidly changing towards the tenseness of the highly populated centres.

But despite the new tenseness in Ickenham's mean streets:

The neighbourhood is one of great loneliness, qualified by a few farm-houses here and there, and no-one wandering through the woods and lanes could believe that he [or she] was within only fifteen miles of the Metropolis. *[ML 1921]*

And this still seems true in 1928:

Ickenham, despite the neighbouring depots of the Royal Air Force, still retains at the centre its old world charm and there are few more typically English villages than this.

But a key event in Ickenham's history has started:

... Swakeleys ... standing in a park of 300 acres, now being developed as a residential estate.

We learn a little more in the housing section, though under "Other Housing Developments" rather than with the Metropolitan estates. Ickenham is

Charmingly situated.

Yes, and

Exceptionally healthy.

In what way?! In any case ...

43

Active housing development [*is*] proceeding on the delightful Swakeleys estate. *[ML 1928]*

According to the 1932 edition:

[*Swakeleys*] is now being developed as a residential estate, but the mansion with some 30 acres of ground was recently acquired by the Foreign Office Sports Association and is used as the country house centre of the Association's athletic and social activities. *[ML 1932]*

And development is spreading.

Active housing development *[is]* proceeding on the delightful Swakeleys Estate and Ivy House Farm Estate.

Back in 1924 Harper is lamenting the fact that

Across country, from Harrow to Uxbridge, by way of Eastcote, Ruislip, and Ickenham, new railways are acting upon the country like the sun upon fruit: they are "ripening" it, as the land agent would say, for building. *[RNR]*

Ten years later, according to Briggs, the fruit has been picked and is in the process of being eaten.

The village green ... at Ickenham is feeling the suburban draught ... and some skill is needed ... to find a viewpoint from which everything in sight is pleasing.

... the agricultural districts of Hillingdon and Ickenham are rapidly transforming themselves into residential suburbs, thereby following the prevailing and apparently inevitable trend of things in the county.

The "quiet village" of Ickenham is now disturbed by a constant thunder of builders' lorries. Opposite the village church you can get a permanent wave or buy gramophone records, or even imbibe "morning coffee".

A suburb indeed, though the need for the quotation marks has been lost over the course of time. Does Briggs feel that "morning coffee" is only for bounders, or possibly the non-U? In any case, there is some good news.

It appears that Swakeleys ... has now escaped its very imminent peril of demolition, and that though rows of "Tudor Homes" are creeping up to it from all sides, the house itself ... is saved for prosperity. Considering the enormous area of still virgin land around it, there seems no reason why such a splendid mansion should ever have been in danger, but it was so. Some land-grabbers seem to have the mentality of a small boy with a catapult. *[MON]*

Holmes develops the theme:

That portion of the County of Middlesex lying between Uxbridge and Harrow was, until a few years ago, the most rural district within a radius of fifteen miles from Charing Cross; but as these pages are being written, hedgerows are disappearing, fields are being intersected by new yellow roads, and the "superior detached residence" is springing up everywhere between the picturesque old villages of Ickenham and Ruislip and the rather shabby west-end of Harrow.

But Ickenham has more class than some, as it

... stands yet unspoilt and rural about its spacious green. "Development" between the village and its station is proceeding apace, though "Jerry" is not in evidence. Some quite charming types of modern domestic architecture are to be seen

45

hereabouts, and the difference between the city man's home here and those a few miles away beside the older railways that were the first to tempt him into the country, is remarkable. *[LC]*

To let Pevsner have the last word:

Like its neighbours, Ruislip and Uxbridge, [*Ickenham*] is a growing place, but keeps some of the semblance of a village ...
[BEM]

I have lived in Ickenham for the last ten years, so it is perhaps more difficult than with Wembley to look at it with a fresh eye. But I am going to have a walk around it and try. I leave my house in Breakspear Road South on a sunny June morning. The traffic is as noisy as usual but in the hayfield on the other side of the road they are completing the cutting, which may or may not do much for my daughter's hay fever. The houses here were put up by a builder called Heath in the early 1950s. They are attractive, many of them detached, in a variety of styles and designed, I feel, to have a slightly rural feel about them. Obviously they are post the actual Metro-land period but I imagine that they were in part sold originally on the fact that they run up to the Green Belt.

I am now at the bottom of Greenacres Avenue and turning into Derwent Avenue. This is where housing development stopped before World War II. Typical suburban semis, but nice ones, and also some bungalows. The roads are tree-lined as one might expect, in line with the Metro-land dream.

Arriving in Swakeleys Road, I stand on the bridge over the so-called River Pinn, in fact a not very large stream. It is fairly clear today and flowing gently. There is some rubbish in it, of course, but it looks pretty, with a moorhen footling around a little upstream. If I walked in that [northerly] direction I would be heading for the open countryside. If I crossed the road and walked through the little strip of woodland beside the river I would come to Swakeleys House. Swakeleys Road itself is a dual carriageway, fairly busy, but pleasant to look at and with lots of trees. In fact it epitomises Ickenham: lots of trees and greenery, too much traffic.

As I walk towards the village the houses are mostly semis, with some detached, and nearly all in good condition, perhaps partly reflecting the fact that approximately half of the adult population appears to consist of builders. In any case, Ickenham is a fairly well-off place, with a predominance of owner occupation and a bastion of Tory voting even in these troubled times for the party. There is not much property here under £250,000.

I cross the road now to what was the main lodge to Swakeleys House; white walls, quite old and a pretty substantial building. Rather olde worlde inside too, as I recall from a Christmas party there some years ago. Next to the wall are the remains of one of the Swakeleys gate posts and beyond is The Avenue, Ickenham's second most prestigious road, protected by a sign saying "Private road. No footpaths. Caution speed ramps. Please drive slowly. Peasants only on business". [I made the last one up, but the intention is clear]. The houses are mostly detached, and large. It is quiet along here at this time of day except for the sound of the birds. All very leafy and pleasant. On the left, set well back, is the former gamekeeper's cottage for the estate; a nice house with a big well-mown lawn and white cast-iron tables and chairs. A good place to sit out if you don't mind being seen from the road. On a beautifully sunny day like this, with just some little white clouds, The Avenue looks at its best.

I am heading for what remains of the Swakeleys grounds, these houses of course being some of those built there from the 1920s onwards. The park itself suffers from the usual problems of litter and vandalism, but today these are not too much in evidence and it looks pretty much as you would expect the grounds of a small stately home to look. I'm standing by the railings at the north end of the lake. The council finally got round to a clean up operation a year ago, the lake having become stagnant and smelly since the Pinn was diverted in the cause of flood prevention. Standing where I am the results don't look too impressive, with plenty of rubbish in the water, including a child's bike. But today is a day for accentuating the positive! The park looks good and although, as I said previously, there are no deer or rabbits here any more, there are plenty of birds of many types, as I can observe whilst slowly jogging through the park in the early mornings. Also badgers and foxes, the latter possibly explaining the absence of rabbits. Across the lake I can see part of the house now, though obviously the view is clearer in the winter, and there is a family of five coot chicks paddling around with mum and dad. Overall it is rather beautiful, and having this in the middle, as well as the countryside round the edges, helps to distinguish Ickenham from a common or garden suburb.

I come out into Swakeleys Drive, not to be confused with Swakeleys Road. Ahead a pretty-looking path continues through the woods leading who knows where. Except that one does know where. It leads to the six lanes of fumes and noise called the A40. Swakeleys Drive was one of the early roads to be developed on the estate in the late 1920s. It has some large detached houses but a lot of semis, some of them extended, with a variety of designs but on the whole giving a fairly harmonious end result. Most of the houses are set pretty well back from what is a rather busy road.

Part way down I arrive at the gates on the south side of Swakeleys. There is still a beautiful grove of trees, which continues on the other side of Swakeleys Drive along a road called, originally enough, The Grove, with nice looking semis behind wide verges leading in the direction of the roar from the A40. As I walk on, the variety of the housing styles

48

becomes even more apparent around Vyners Way, a rather twee close running into the Swakeleys grounds with a backdrop of fine trees, and houses verging on the gingerbread. On the corner is a definite gingerbread house, with lilac shutters with hearts in them and what can only be described as a real cottage garden. [I see in the *Uxbridge Leader* a few days later that the house is for sale through Swakeleys Estates: "A unique and charming cottage style semi detached in a most sought after corner plot location". A snip at £399,950.]

I could turn towards the village along Court Road, another pleasant thoroughfare on the Swakeleys Estate, but I decide instead to go along Long Lane, busy and noisy even mid morning. On my left are some large detached houses and on my right some real Tudorbethan semis, with next to them a couple of cottages from the 19th century, a remnant of truly rural Ickenham, which have been refurbished in recent years with some new houses next to them but not spoiling them.

I have now reached the Douay Martyrs School, a Roman Catholic establishment that was rather controversial locally at one time, with the air at IRA meetings thick with complaints about the behaviour of some of the students [one shop even had a sign saying "No Douay Martyrs pupils served"!] and counter-accusations of sectarianism. Perhaps part of the problem was that, unlike the other schools, most of the pupils are not from the village. In Ickenham we like things to be local. Even the yobs. Happily these problems now seem to be in the past. I ought to mention here that I received a very courteous note from Mrs Geraldine Davies, the current head teacher, in response to one from me concerning a copy of the 1987 reprint of *Metro-land* that I bought in Brighton, containing the inscription: "To Lord Hailsham with gratitude, from the Sixth Form at the Douay Martyrs School". Apparently he had participated in a Sixth Form seminar programme.

The school is housed in hideous 1960s-style buildings, overflowing its site and with a forest of [dangerous?] telecoms

49

masts on the roof. I start to walk alongside the school, up an old lane which looks rather inviting and shady. As I walk I catch sight of fields on the left with houses on the Glebe Estate in the background, marooned in fields by the passing of Green Belt legislation. So in a way they continue to meet the promise of a home in the countryside, albeit that some of the fields are rather scrubby with just a few horses grazing. A little further on is a functioning farm [Long Lane Farm] with geese pottering around at the front and hanging baskets of flowers. A pleasantly rural scene only slightly spoilt by [again] the roar of the A40. I believe originally this was all to have been developed but fortunately that didn't happen. I now reach the remains of the moat of the Manor Farm, and read a sign announcing that it [the moat not the house] is owned by Douay Martyrs. It is next to the Manor House itself, which is apparently mostly 14th century and is therefore one of the oldest buildings in Ickenham. I could walk quite a long way here through fields on which agriculture has given up and which have been designated a nature reserve, but I am heading through the Glebe Estate, perhaps not the prettiest part of Ickenham, but described by the estate agents as "ever popular" when offering 3 bed semis for £250 + K.

I am standing in front of a rather run-down row of shops, one boarded up, another describing itself as "Off Licence, Supermarket, Video Agent and seller of fireworks", and a "tyre and battery specialist", with what appears to be a small scrap yard across the road. Then I notice two pairs of cottages, one dated 1893, thus preceding the opening of the nearby Met station in 1905 and representing an early stage of [very small time] development. Progressing towards the Met line I pass on my right the Compass Theatre, which joins on to another of Ickenham's older preserved buildings, Ickenham Hall. There is a small piece of green space between it and the line, with a lady walking her dog. Green is Ickenham's colour.

I am now in the middle of the village, next to the distinctive shelter over the pump, "erected in memory of Charlotte Gell in the year 1866". It appears that the well was also sunk at that time but I don't know what they did for water before that. I am surrounded by some of the older buildings in the village, with St Giles' church opposite me, the Coach and Horses behind me [its distinctive sign sadly replaced with the bland emblem of Ember Inns] and next to the pond. The elements would seem all to be as 100 years ago, except that it is also a busy T junction and any temptation to stop for a gossip would probably be defeated by the noise. Also, on one side of Swakeleys Road are the shops, a jumble of architectural styles with no very pleasing overall effect, and certainly not a rural one. At this point Long Lane becomes Ickenham High Road and I am going to walk along it to the boundary at West Ruislip station.

I pass another oldish building, Pete Cottage, and what was until recently the Ickenham Garden Centre, closed in controversial circumstances because some office developer wants to deprive us of a little more of our heritage. On the other side of the road is the start of the US Navy base, on the site of the old aircraft works. One wonders why the Americans thought this a suitable spot for the Navy. Did they envisage a flotilla of Red warships steaming up the River Pinn? In any case, this part of Ickenham has long been a little corner of the ol' USA, baseball diamond and all, with the villagers invited in every 4th of July to help celebrate the defeat of our ancestors. Now, however, the Yankee sea dogs are setting sail for Uxbridge-sur-Mer and the land will be turned over to building, an infinitely preferable alternative to any renewed assault on the green fields.

Opposite the base is the little old Congregational chapel, dating from 1835 and replaced by a new church when the population grew in the 1930s, but still just about standing and in use as a "recycling centre" [junk yard]. The Soldier's Return pub and the cottages nearby are of similar date. Then there are some houses [villas!] of Edwardian vintage, one pair

51

with an interesting wooden balcony, and a row of shops significantly called "Great Central Parade". Significantly, because this is where development in Ickenham started, near the line linking Marylebone with Birmingham and beyond, and not round the Met station. The Greenway here was the first road in the new Ickenham, 100 years ago.

I am walking up towards West Ruislip station, which is on the boundary between little Ickenham and the Big Smoke of Ruislip. There is a fair bit of rivalry here and I fondly recall the manifesto of a lady standing for a position of Parent Governor at Breakspear, my daughter's junior school. The lady had been born in Ickenham but her wicked parents took her away to Ruislip. Fortunately, after getting married she had been able to return to Ickenham and had lived here ever since. My wife and I labelled her "rolling stone". In any case, this is the only place where Ickenham almost joins on to somewhere else. Standing on the railway bridge and looking approximately north I can see trees and fields very close by, though I believe that originally the plan was to continue development through to South Harefield, where a passenger station was opened, and subsequently shut when the houses did not get built.

I am now going back into the centre of the village to record some further observations there, but I know that if I turned up Oak Avenue on the right I would first come to the cricket club and then be able to walk through the fields pretty well back to my house. It is more obvious in some places than others, but in Ickenham you are never far from countryside, or at least open space.

Escaping from a scruffy patch of small office buildings [some empty and vandalised, so why do they want to build more?] I decide to go through the church yard, which is well maintained and, judging by both it and the church itself, time might well have stood still, except [of course] for the traffic noise. As the church is open I pop in. A real village church, with a list of rectors from 1335 and a plethora of memorials to former leading families, most notably the various branches of the Clarkes.

Turning up Swakeleys Road, once you move away from the church the initial impression is of a rather untidy scene, with cars parked and double parked in front of the [architecturally] undistinguished shops. Not much like a village. However, passing the village hall [like many things here, a product of the inter-war period] as a stranger you would get a pleasant surprise, for across the dual carriageway appears a row of cottages including alms houses and one more substantial old building, currently available for sale ["a charming 18th century Grade 2 listed cottage with extensive potential!"] for a mere £599,950. Very nice it looks too.

So what makes Ickenham different from [say] Wembley? It is perhaps not so much the way it was developed as the fact that it was made to stop developing. Without the Green Belt and the war, how far would the houses have stretched? To Beaconsfield? Wycombe? Of course there was no stadium here. Not so much as a cinema. It was always a backwater, and please God it always will be.

Further reading

The Story of Ickenham Morris W. Hughes, Hillingdon Borough Libraries, 1983

Bygone Ruislip and Uxbridge Dennis F. Edwards, Phillimore, 1985

Britain in Old Photographs, Ruislip, Ickenham & District Dennis F. Edwards, Sutton Publishing, 1996

Ickenham & Harefield Past Eileen M. Bowlt, Historical Publications, 1996

The Archive Photographs Series, Around Ruislip Maria Newbery, Carolynne Cotton, Julie Ann Packham and Gwyn Jones, Chalford, 1996

3

"Ruislip for the quiet English countryside"

Although from the perspective of Ickenham folk Ruislip represents the Big City, and for people further afield the name is redolent of Acacia Avenue [there really is one here], to this 1950s Wembley boy a trip to the Lido meant a taste of countryside and seaside rolled into one. But does living here feel like living in the countryside? When I set out later to explore, I will be taking a view myself, but a glance at the map gives the initial answer that at least to some extent it will depend on which part of Ruislip is in question. To the west is open countryside and to the north a remnant of the ancient Middlesex Forest, but to the east it is houses all the way to Harrow and to the south lie the delights of Yeading and Hayes. In 1876 its rural credentials are not in doubt:

> Ruislip is pleasantly situated in a quiet rural district, between low uplands, watered by the two head branches of the Isleworth river, and backed by Ruislip Park, Wood and Reservoir. The occupations are agricultural; much of the land is devoted to pasture, and there is considerable trade in timber and firewood.

So the fields and woods provide people with a living, but also [at least for some of them] with sport:

> Ruislip Park, N. of the village, is a famous fox-hunting meet. *[HEL]*

If the Ruislip of 2003 is anything like Ickenham, this hunt ought to be re-formed before the Government ban takes effect and both "villages" are overrun by the Red Menace.

Returning to the late 19th century, Foley points out that that the attractions are not just natural ones:

> Ruislip village, which stands on a hill ...

Does it? It is certainly not very apparent today. A little poetic licence, perhaps? In any case, the village

> ... has a veritable bygone look. The church is one of the largest village churches in Middlesex, and seems, as we look around us, many times too big for the present demands upon its space.

Perhaps the builders of this cathedral foresaw something that Foley did not! The population certainly caught up with it, though I do not know how many of them use it for their Sunday devotions nowadays. And Nature was close by:

> ... we gain charming glimpses between the trees of the beautiful Ruislip Lake. It has a lonely situation, flanked by wooded hills, no road passing by it; and we learn without surprise that it is the haunt of many rarer kinds of wild birds. *[OLM]*

Close to the turn of the century, Walford points out that Ruislip is not only rural, but isolated. It is

> ... a remote and straggling village, four miles from every railway station, and therefore most primitive.

Four miles away from a station and without cars, the railway might indeed have been on another planet. But what does he mean by calling it "primitive"? It sounds as if the natives were

56

living in mud huts and dancing round camp fires with bones in their noses, but presumably he is saying that as of 1898 Ruislip had been spared the benefits of modern development. Even so it was much bigger than Ickenham, but with a fairly scattered population, that was considered to include Eastcote and Northwood.

> Out of its entire population of some fifteen hundred souls, only a hundred or so live round the original village green, now an open roadway, on the eastern side of which stands the finest village church in all Middlesex, Harrow only excepted.

And rather than mud huts there are

> ... some picturesque church houses, which show by their projecting timbers that they have stood there for centuries.

Now he spells it out:

> Owing to its remote situation Ruislip has undergone but little change for many generations.

But isolation has not shielded it from general rural trends.

> The demand for hay in the metropolis has slowly but surely brought about the extinction of arable farming in this locality, and so only a few acres remain under cultivation. This would have been a sad misfortune to the poorer inhabitants, but it is compensated by a new industry which has sprung up, that of sorting and cutting up firewood, of which the supply is inexhaustible. This occupies the women and children as well as the cottars.

So the woodland gives the Ruislip poor advantages over those in other Middlesex villages, and in addition

The poor, in compensation for their ancient common lands, have the right of turning their cattle out to graze on certain meadows at Ruislip and Eastcote.

Walford describes the modern-day Lido in rather prosaic terms, whilst pointing out some sporting benefits.

The reservoir on Ruislip Common extends from Cannon's Bridge for nearly a mile towards Rickmansworth. It covers an area of 80 acres, and belongs to the Grand Junction Canal Company, who use it to supply the deficiency caused by the waste of water in working their canal. The reservoir is much frequented by anglers.

But it appears that Basil Brush is now safe:

Ruislip Park, which bounds the village on the east, and is intersected by a public footpath, covers upwards of forty acres of land, and is laid out with picturesque drives, and ornamented by rare old timber. It used to be a famous foxhunting meet. [GL]

Writing in 1906, Firth can still describe an entirely rural scene.

Ruislip is a pretty village, lying secluded in the level plain between Harrow and Uxbridge, with fine woods to the N. between it and Northwood.

Note "level plain". It is not just me and the Ordnance Survey map denying that Ruislip is on a hill!

The village itself now consists of a cluster of picturesque houses and inns at the cross-roads, with the tower of the church showing above the roofs, and the big outbuildings of a large farm on the other side of the road.

The church *[St Martin]* is an interesting old building, and most charmingly situated, for the well-kept churchyard is surrounded on two sides by the half-timbered backs of old cottages, and on the other two by the open fields.

The manor farm, to the north of the church, belongs to King's College, Cambridge. Traces of its old moat may be seen from the road by the brook side.

Ruislip Park, on the E. side of the village, is bisected by a foot-path to the hamlet of Kingsend. ... To the north of Ruislip flows the brook Pin, from Eastcote and Pinner – at the bridge a pleasant footpath leads to Eastcote, skirting the wood – and beyond are the Park Wood and the hamlet of Bury Street, on the road to Northwood. There is also a footpath through the wood, which, especially in the spring, is well worth a visit. The Ruislip Reservoir lies to the north of the road, and narrows towards Northwood. ... One of the feeders – often quite dry – winds through the fields most pleasantly from near Ruislip to Ickenham, and has a footpath at its side. Another small hamlet, Ruislip Common, lies to the south of the reservoir. A widish tract of open common ground on its N and W sides is known as Poor's Field, beyond which are more woods, extending to Northwood itself. These are private, but they are skirted by the high-road, which rises 150 feet up Duck's Hill, before dropping down to Northwood. *[MF]*

A year later Hope Moncrieff confirms the cosy rustic picture, and not only mentions the Met [extended through Ruislip in 1904] for the first time, but warns of its inevitable impact.

The village of Ruislip stands to the south of Park Wood, where the church shows its flint tower set on a rise among fat farms, beside the course of the brook we have followed from Eastcote. The churchyard commands a pleasant prospect over swells of wood and meadow, that fall to duller aspects, cut off by the Metropolitan branch passing to the south of the village.

By a passage beside the picturesque old "Swan" opposite the Church, there is a way across Ruislip Park, on whose privacy the builder has set seals of doom. *[MFH]*

The rapid speed of change, certainly compared with Ickenham, is shown only a year later [1908] by *Where to Live Round London.* The village is already becoming a touch suburban.

A small cluster of houses – some of them ancient and timbered – two or three small inns, a few shops, and behind the houses a large and beautiful mediaeval church, judiciously restored and well kept; such is even to-day the centre of this peaceful village. It has become, however, the nucleus of what is already a pleasant residential quarter, steadily growing in size and in favour with those who are enquiring where to live close to the metropolis.

And the reasons?

The factors that have contributed, and are contributing, to this change are as follows. First, its healthy and agreeable situation, surrounded as it is by beautiful woods and pleasant undulating uplands of open country. Secondly, several considerable tracts of land have come into the market and are being developed in an enterprising manner as building estates, consisting mainly of good class residences. Notable amongst these estates is the Ruislip Park Estate, which consists of a beautiful old park with fine timber, most of which is left standing, and where houses of high class are being built. Then, Ruislip has ceased to be rural as regards its government, being now associated with a neighbouring residential locality under the Ruislip-Northwood Urban District Council. Lastly, and this, of course, is very important to business and professional men engaged in London

60

during the daytime, – Ruislip is singularly fortunate as regards railway facilities, as it is served by three railway companies and two conveniently situated stations.

This is of course a publication with a purpose, and the text is echoed in the advertisement for the Ruislip Park Estate:

> This delightful old world park of about 40 acres is now being developed as a high-class Building Estate, great care being taken as to the class of house erected.
>
> The Estate is cut up into half-acre plots and nearly all the fine old timber has been saved, adding materially to the beauty of the Estate.
>
> The situation of Ruislip is high, and the surrounding scenery fine ...
>
> Plots of all sizes are for sale at reasonable prices, or would be let on Building Leases, and there are constantly newly erected houses that are available for letting.

That these are early days is indicated by letting being given at least equal prominence with buying, and the "high class" nature of the estate is confirmed by the saving of the "fine old timber". The simple rule of thumb emerging is that the more money you have, the more rural a feel to your surroundings.

A year later, in 1909, Jerrold appears to indicate that this early building has not had a great impact on the "feel" of Ruislip.

> Here is a pretty old village street, with irregular gabled buildings about the cross roads near the church, some admirable ancient cottages, especially the half-timbered backs seen from the churchyard, and a fine flint and stone church, the embattled tower of which shows above the roofs.

Though the railway passes along the south of the village, and there is building going on, Ruislip remains an unspoiled village, representative of many such Middlesex villages of a few years ago. How countrified are its immediate surroundings may be recognised by such a sight as I had on first visiting it, when I met two men with broad deep hampers on their backs, flowing over with the massed blooms of wild hyacinths, and forming an unforgettable point of colour in the village street. These flowers had been gathered – not, it is probable, without trespass – from the woods in the neighbourhood, and were evidently being taken to be sold door to door in the London suburbs, or at City kerbstones.

There is perhaps a suggestion here that Jerrold's picture of Ruislip had been formed at an even earlier time, but he does at least acknowledge that delightful surroundings do not free [most] people of the need to work for a living.

Certainly in the matter of woodland Ruislip is one of the more favoured of our county's districts. To the north stretch hundreds of acres of woods, on either side of the broad extent of Ruislip Reservoir. Seen on the western side, from the road leading to the Northwood footpath, the fine sheet of water, backed by masses of trees, looks like some Canadian lake of the woods. Along the southern fringe of this woodland – between it and the little Pin is a delightful footpath way to the attractive hamlet of Eastcote, while another passes through the wood. From Eastcote again a pleasant way, partly by footpath, may be followed over Haste Hill to Northwood, from near which we may hark back, still by footpath, over Poor Field, near the reservoir, to the little hamlet of Ruislip Common, and so to Ruislip again. Such a walk gives us many delightful bits of the varied scenery of this favoured corner of Middlesex, and it is but one of the many pleasant walks that may be made with Ruislip as a centre.

The great reservoir – about 80 acres in extent – lying as it does in a little-frequented district, is probably the resort of many uncommon aquatic birds .... The angling ... is strictly preserved for the members of a small club, but the fortunate few by whom it is fished frequently catch, I am told, "specimen" tench and occasionally very large pike.

This north-western corner of Middlesex offers some of the most beautifully rural bits that the county has left to show. [HBI]

So Ruislip is left in [fairly] rural isolation in the run up to, and for the duration of, "the war that will end all war", and we take up the story again with *Metro-land* in 1921. Ruislip's twin claims on the attentions of that publication's readers are quickly spelt out:

Ruislip, in common with that beautiful part of Middlesex in which it lies, makes two appeals to the Londoner. One is expressed in its charms as a holiday resort; ...

This side is revealed, more than in the case of Ickenham, by the listings at the back:

The Orchard Bungalow: "It's really in an orchard". Adult parties catered for. Luncheons, Teas etc.

The Poplars: superior accommodation for Parties up to 200 at reasonable terms. Delightful sit. Picturesque Tea Gardens.

And last, but apparently by no means least:

Kingsend Farm: Ideal for School Treats and Large Parties. Accomodation for 2000. Permanent buildings.

Here we are clearly looking at tripperdom on some scale, with the early cyclists augmented by the Metropolitan hordes.

63

Perhaps for many it was their first visit to this lovely village and countryside, planting in their minds its other potential as

> ... a place of residence. Prior to that fateful event which has enveloped Europe in gloom, Ruislip was progressing very rapidly. But the cruel energies of war absorbed the whole strength of the nation, and the Garden City and other settlements planned in Ruislip were arrested just as they were on the point of developing. Under peace conditions it is to be trusted that this interrupted activity will be resumed. *[ML 1921]*

Now we are cutting to the chase. "It is to be trusted" indeed! Whatever the number of day trippers, they mostly came at the weekends and some of them perhaps only once a year if they were lucky. What was needed was the steady, captive market of the season ticket holder for the City. So, let's get building, though initially on a modest scale. By 1928 *Metro-land* can record happily that

> Ruislip Park, on the east side of the main street, has been covered with pleasant villa houses, and the little township is growing rapidly in all directions.

Oddly, according to my map Ruislip Park was on the *west* side of the High Street, though this reference to east only seems to be following earlier writers. In any case, there is more development afoot:

> Between Ruislip and the next village of Ickenham, beyond what was once the hamlet of Kingsend, are large depots of the Royal Air Force.

But without, apparently, loss of the old charms.

> Ruislip has several tea gardens, some with recreation grounds attached, which are popular places of resort in the Summer

64

time. There are pleasant lanes on the north side of Ruislip, beyond the hamlet of Bury-street, where the ground rises to Duck's Hill and Copse Wood, and the whole district towards Harefield and Northwood is most attractive.

The advertisements show the increasing pace of development, on two sites near the centre of the village, both in fact on the east side of the High Street. As usual, they offer rural tranquillity *and* proximity to the station and shops.

Pinn View Estate: Well built and perfectly equipped houses ... In an ideal position within 8 minutes of Ruislip Station, adjoining open spaces and overlooking the River Pinn and Ruislip Woods, high ground. The houses have been specially planned with a view to giving FOUR bedrooms at a price usually charged for three. ... £915 leasehold. Freehold can be obtained.

Church Croft Estate: Before deciding – visit Church Croft. Superior Well-Built Houses with accommodation for garages are now being erected at Church Croft from £1000 freehold .... Church Croft is situate in the delightful old world village of Ruislip with its woodlands, commons, lakes and farm land surroundings and yet within a few minutes' walk of station and shops.

The Orchard has changed too. The emphasis has moved away from Sunday School treats and day trippers towards the features of an hotel, with a reminder that we are as yet still only in 1927 coming from the trumpeting of electric light:

The Orchard Bungalow: Private Residential Hotel in an orchard and adjoins golf course. Telephone; garage; electric light. *[ML 1928]*

The 1932 edition has news of yet more houses, with the Manor Farm Estate being true Metro-land.

The Manor Farm Estate of some 64 acres, adjoining many hundreds of acres of permanently preserved woodland and a large recreation park, is in course of development by the Metropolitan Railway Country Estates Ltd. Another new estate, Ruislip Station Estate, is being opened up on the south side of the Metropolitan line.

The ad for the Manor Farm Estate rather gives the game away by mentioning previous development but can still promise country views, as well as a quintessentially suburban "recreation park".

Manor Farm Estate: The land fronting the main Eastcote-Ruislip road having been disposed of, the 50 odd acres at the rear have been developed, giving access to some valuable Free-hold Building Sites. ... These Plots enjoy unusual and extensive views of permanently preserved well-wooded and undulating country, and in addition there is a large area reserved for a Recreation Park, on to which a considerable section of the land abuts.

Despite his low prices, H.L. Bowers is not to be outdone with his promises of country surroundings, good climate and clean air combined with modern amenities, south of the tracks:

H.L. Bowers, Ruislip Station Estate: At last – a "quality" house at low cost. Here is your chance – seize it! A real worth-while "quality" seven-room house for £695 Freehold. ... The Ruislip Station Estate, on which these delightful houses are located, has everything in its favour. It can be reached from Town, in less time than it takes to read your evening paper. On all sides are green fields and pleasant hedgerows. The climate is mild and equable; the air is healthy and invigorating, while unlimited facilities for outdoor recreation obtain and particularly liberal educational and shopping facilities exist.

66

Later, under "Other Housing Developments", *Metro-land* says that

> Extensive private building operations [*are*] proceeding in all directions. *[ML 1932]*

And no tea gardens are shown in the "List of Hotels, Caterers, Etc.". Ruislip the tourist spot has given way to Ruislip the suburb.

Back in 1924, Harper is able to wax lyrical about the old, isolated, Ruislip:

> Ruislip is a very queer, old world place, that until quite recently was actually four miles from a railway station, but has now acquired a station of its very own, and seems rather sleepily surprised at the fact.

> How picturesque the village of Ruislip is, let the illustrations in these pages show. In one you are looking across to the church, whose grey battlemented tower rises behind a finely massed group of old cottage roofs and chimneys. The signboard of the "George" inn, standing on its post in the middle of the village street, is surmounted by some good old wrought iron-work, and the post itself is more covered with arms, directing to many surrounding places, and with various notices of a more or less commercial character, than any other post the present writer, in much travelling, ever remembers to have seen. *[RNR]*

Coming forward to 1932, *London and Suburbs Old and New* wants, as in the pages of *Metro-land* itself, to link this tradition with aggressive modernity [a cinema] and claim an harmonious end result.

> Few places more happily unite a pleasing sense of old-world repose and modern development than does the charming old

village of Ruislip, for here the age-old and the ultra-new appear to merge into a most harmonious juxtaposition.

The historic church and encircling cottages carry history and tradition back for hundreds of years; whilst in complete accord the modern store and cinema assure the comfort and pleasure demanded by the modern spirit of efficiency and ease.

I will be assessing later how these promises look in central Ruislip today, but the authors make some bold claims for Ruislip Manor and South Ruislip too.

Ruislip Manor may justly claim to be the most accessible and the least spoiled of the residential districts round London. It can be reached in less time than it takes to read your evening paper, and it has just that quiet reserve with that degree of friendliness which will make you want to live there for always. If you have been hesitating where to make your home, you need hesitate no longer.

What is all this? How can a district have "quiet reserve"? Does it mean the residents are all incomers who do not know each other? It goes on in a way that epitomises the dream:

On all sides are green fields; close at hand are health-giving woods ...; you will find houses ready to live in which are reasonable in cost, or land for building a house to your own individual taste. In a word, nothing is lacking that is required to make a perfect residential district.

Moreover, apart from the definite attractions of Ruislip Manor, there is a "something" about the district that is irresistible. It may be its assurance of charm, the freshness of its air, or its settled look of ancient peace. Whatever it be, it suggests a new standard of home life; it confirms your sudden conviction that this is the place of your desire.

68

Even the writer[s] of *Metro-land* might have blushed to pen such stuff, not least the overlooking of any possible impact of development on the "settled look of ancient peace". Essential development such as shops:

> A fine parade of shops is to be erected in Parkway, facing the railway station; thus in the near future the Estate will possess a shopping centre of its own.

South Ruislip also gets the treatment:

> This is a very delightful modern residential settlement ... .Its elevation [standing, as it does, at an altitude of about 120 to 140 feet above sea level], with a subsoil of loam, surrounded by a beautiful stretch of open country, free from anything sugges- tive of overcrowding, give to this charming spot an inestimable value for residential purposes, and for those who desire fresh, pure air, bracing climate and rural peace it can be highly recommended.

What an Arcadia! Plus sporting and other open air attrac- tions:

> ... Northolt Park, with its beautiful racecourse, is within five minutes walk. ...

> There are delightful country walks; in fact all the healthy advantages of the open country at your door. Yet in the space of minutes one is in the largest towns.

> Could anyone desire better facilities? And for those desiring all that goes towards happiness and contentment, we would advise this particular locality for permanent residence. *[LAS]*

As we have found before, and will again, Briggs gives a counter view to that of the salesman, though in an apparently balanced and objective way. He is complimentary about the planners of Ruislip proper.

This urban district ... contains some of the most charming, unspoiled rural scenery in Middlesex, and, what is almost equally important nowadays, its inhabitants have had the foresight to safeguard its beauties for posterity, so far as is reasonably possible. The district ... was one of the first in England to adopt the provisions of the Town Planning Act of 1909, and ten years later the "Ruislip Association" was formed "to discuss and take action upon local matters affecting the proper development of the district and, in particular, the preservation of its amenities". ... It is therefore due to the vision and civic sense of a small group of intelligent people that Ruislip has not gone the way of most of suburban Middlesex, and has not yet succumbed entirely to the strident propaganda that has vulgarised so much of "Metroland".

He accepts development, provided that it is properly controlled. Metro-land cannot be left to its own devices! In any case, as he heads south he starts to worry.

A perambulation of the area to-day reveals an enormous activity in building, especially in the southern part of the district.

The south part of the district, that is, south of the District [*It seems that he prefers not to say the word "Metropolitan", though it was the first on the tracks!*] Railway ... is an area almost square in shape, measuring nearly two miles in each direction, and is practically barren of natural charms. Its contours are negligible, its trees scarce, and the few farms and barns that still survive are not of outstanding interest. A large aerodrome, with its characteristically "useful" buildings, occupies part of the ground ... and soon the extension of Western Avenue will cross the south-western corner. Already a squalid colony of

70

huts and shacks has grown up around Northolt Junction *[now South Ruislip]*, signs of intense activity are evident elsewhere, and the tide of "Distinctive Homes" is beginning to sweep relentlessly southward from the District Railway, which has already opened an additional station to cope with the hundreds of misguided folk who think that they are going to live in the country. It is true that even an occasional ploughman can be seen in this district, but the few remaining cultivated fields have not long to live and he knows it. The district is awaiting the glad time when every acre will carry its full quota of twelve "Baronial Halls". This tract of roughly four square miles seems certain to be built up, and as it has no natural features or perceptible contours, it will be a depressing district unless some really imaginative plan of lay-out be adopted. It is true that a considerable part of the rather dreary banks of the Yeading Brook has been acquired as open space, but neither that reservation nor the recreation grounds also bought are very stimulating to the lover of beautiful landscape. They will provide space in which to breathe and play games: that is all.

Can this really be the same area that occasioned the purple prose of *London and Suburbs*? One notes in particular the reference to the "misguided folk who think that they are going to live in the country". Briggs is happier back up north.

But the central part of the urban district, the part which contains Ruislip village, Eastcote village, Ruislip Reservoir and its girdle of woods, is so beautiful that the council has done well to concentrate its resources on preserving as much as possible from obliteration. There is already a great deal of building between the District *[again!]* Railway and the Eastcote-Ruislip-Ickenham road, but much of it is excellently designed and practically all of it is well laid out. This part of the parish is pleasantly undulating, rising to 300 feet at Haste Hill on one side of the reservoir, and slightly more at Copse Hill on the other side

71

.... This fine expanse of water ... approaches the appearance of a natural lake as nearly as any reservoir can do. ... It is beautiful at any time of year, especially on a quiet winter afternoon when summer visitors are not making merry on the lake and when the flocks of wildfowl are undisturbed. ... It is to be hoped that it will never be vulgarised by speed-boats ... *[like the]* Welsh Harp. Pylons carrying the "grid" transmission-wires somewhat mar the view looking south, but in Middlesex one cannot avoid these things. There is a group of modern cottages at the south end, but, like most other buildings in this enlightened neighbourhood, they are designed with taste and restraint. East of the reservoir a magnificent tract of open space has been secured for ever .... This *[includes]* the lovely sylvan stretch known as Park Wood, purchased in 1933. This is an authentic fragment of the forest of Middlesex ... mentioned in Domesday as "a park of wild beasts of the forest". Its trees are mainly oaks and silver birches. Across the reservoir is the "Poor's Field", with an area of 30 acres, scheduled in the Town-Planning Scheme as a private open space.

He makes a plea for the protection of the woods on the western side as well.

... this is undoubtedly one of the most beautiful spots remaining in the county – indeed, one of the few places left where the ancient charm of Middlesex landscape, hardly changed since the Middle Ages, still remains.

Modernity is not going to retreat.

The latest improvements in transport by which Tube trains from Cockfosters ... run through ... to Eastcote, Ruislip and Uxbridge ... cannot fail to encourage the already active state of building development in the district.

72

But much of the old remains, and even the new is better than elsewhere.

> Near the church stands the old Manor Farm, an ancient building with two large barns, one of which is perhaps the second finest in the county . . . .

> . . . the district also contains a number of really charming half-timbered farms and barns, the former mainly with white-washed brick filling and tiled roofs, the latter with tarred weatherboarding and thatched or tiled roofs. Among them may be mentioned Woodman's Farm in Bury Street, Hill Farm, Shirley's Farm, Green Farm, Mill Farm and "The Barns" at Eastcote.

> As already remarked, the standard of new building in Ruislip is far above the average, thanks to wise direction and artistic taste. Even the shops along the High Street are less blatant than usual, and the new Post Office is charming. *[MON]*

Martin S. Briggs loves Ruislip, as long as he stays on the right [north] side of the tracks!

Just after World War Two, Clunn shows that the process of suburbanisation is complete:

> . . . the old world village of Ruislip, which of late years has become the nucleus of a modern garden suburb . . . .

> The new residential quarter and handsome shopping centre lies mainly to the east of the village and there is also a Rivoli cinema.

And there is more activity in the south.

> South Ruislip is a new residential suburb which has sprung up of late years near Northolt Airport. *[This]* extends for some

distance along the north side of Western Avenue ... . It is mainly used for the Continental services and is of less importance than London Airport. The public are admitted during the summer months at a fee of sixpence and refreshments are served in a large marquee in the absence of a permanent tea house. Small planes seating eight persons convey visitors on a fifteen minutes' pleasure flight over Central London for a fee of fifteen shillings each passenger. *[TFL]*

This reminder of the sometime civilian use of what is now called RAF Northolt is something that most residents probably prefer to forget, in an era when it is spasmodically mentioned as a possible solution to the eternal overcrowding at Heathrow. Opinion amongst local people tends to favour its maintenance as open space for the use of mainly light aircraft, including those ferrying VIPs such as the Prime Minister, even if many of them did not vote for him.

But *The King's England* is more interested in the old Ruislip, and likes what it sees.

Modern houses and shops there are in plenty here, but part of the old village remains, gathered round its fine old church as if seeking protection from an invader. Modern Ruislip, if it is an invader, is a friendly one, and a pleasing example of the new in harmony with the old.

Henry the Sixth gave the manor to King's College Cambridge, and a few years ago the College gave back to Ruislip for preservation the farm, its outbuildings, the old cottages which once served as the post office and nine acres of land, all now in charge of the Office of Works.

It was a great inspiration to turn *[one of the manor farm barns]* into the public library, where Ruislip folk can handle books and read them in an old-world atmosphere.

Back in the busy street we see the grey tower of the church

74

rising above a row of old cottages with cream walls and mellow tiles, standing in gardens, the other old dwellings turned into shops. Sandwiched between these shops is the lychgate, through which we pass as to another world. Here, in the churchyard of lawn and trees and flowers, we see the timbered overhanging storeys of the backs of the houses we have left, and another row of dwellings whose strip of garden is one with that of the church. *[KEM]*

And Pevsner can still find what he wants.

The village with its church, almshouses, and moated farm is now so closely surrounded on all sides by suburban developments that the small and fairly completely preserved nucleus of old building comes as a surprise from whatever direction it is approached. *[BEM]*

For my walkabout, I start right at the centre of things, in the car park at the Manor Farm, on a bright and sunny day in mid October. On the other side I can see some of the outbuildings, which have been converted to modern uses, and the remains of the moat and the mound on which the original motte and bailey castle sat [possibly, according to distinguished local historian Eileen Bowlt!]. It is all very beautiful. On my right I can see the roofs of some white, detached Metro-land houses, and ahead the mellow red brick of the Manor Farm house nestling amongst the trees. Entering the farm yard, I can see how well the old buildings have been adapted. One of the barns has been converted to a library, suffering a little from some idiot graffiti at the moment [a serious problem in this area as sadly it is in so many others] and one of the smaller buildings is labelled as the Cow Byre and houses an art gallery and a café. There is a sign pointing out amongst other things that the Great Barn [closed today but often used for jumble sales and similar events] is the oldest building on the site [built about 1295] and is one of the oldest wooden buildings in the country. The little barn dates from before 1600 and was opened as a public library in 1937. There is real history here surrounding the old dears choosing their library books, and jumblers do their stuff in a building that is 700 years old.

·I have just gone out for a moment on to Bury Street, the old [and current] road to Northwood, to see the business side of the Great Barn, with its huge metal-bound doors. It really is a fine building and, despite the fact that I have lived in the area for some time and been into it on many occasions, I may not ever have looked at it properly before. Going back into the farm yard area, and turning to avoid looking at some more graffiti defacing the library [shame that the perpetrator never learned to read] I see something which, if I ever did know it was here, I had certainly forgotten. There is a little notice saying that these gravestones were salvaged from the former Dogs' Cemetery at St Catherine's Farm in Howletts Lane. The stones include "Peter, a cocker spaniel, died 19th January 1927, the best and truest of friends, the sun in our face the wind in our eyes." So there's one that didn't live to see the development of Ruislip reach its zenith! Another one: "In memory of the black corded [?] poodle dog Pierrot [Japan] which passed away in 1916 of heart failure". Quite a year for death, that one. There are others as well. On one I can just see the name Dodie, but no more.

As I walk back into the farm yard en route to the house itself, I can hear the bell of St Martin's over to my right. It really is lovely here, with the beautiful trees with their changing leaves and the house, pebbledashed below but half-timbered above. I check later in Pevsner and find that the timber framing is from around 1500, not really the subject of this book but another reminder that there is real history here. Walking back is something of an anti-climax as I am looking at the car park and very conscious of the traffic in the High

Street, but on my right is the bowling green with a couple of chaps working on it [I believe that this is where the haystacks used to stand] and behind this a nice old house, painted white and then a little further on the duck pond, still with ducks, along with bicycle frames and similar detritus.

Passing the War Memorial on the way to the church I notice the name of Piper [P.W.]. Not a relative as far as I know, with our Pipers, like many others, tending to come from Sussex. This causes me to stop and look around and I see beyond the Metro-land houses a first line of trees and behind them the ancient forest itself. Very Ruislip!

St Martin's Church yard contains some aged gravestones and yew trees and is surrounded by old cottages. It has a real country feel and *looks* very peaceful. The emphasis is on looks because it *sounds* very noisy! Once on the High Street I can look at the fronts of the cottages, some of which are shops or restaurants, including one currently known as Pizza Organic though it has a tendency to change its name every few years. Across the road is the Swan, one of the older pubs and I have to say looking rather inviting even this early in the morning. I cross over and go into a road called The Oaks to see the first "modern" housing development, the Ruislip Park Estate. One does not get much of an impression at first because there are some rather modern buildings, including the police station on the left, one of those archetypically naff 60s/70s buildings of no visible merit. Once I get past that I start to see the real thing; substantial detached houses, nice hedges and a certain number of old trees, though perhaps not quite as many as I had expected from the originally advertised claims about retaining the old timber. As I walk along Church Avenue I can see an oak to my left but most of the trees are of a rather suburban variety. This estate must have caused quite a stir when it was built and it is still attractive now, though it suffers from problems stemming from being so close to the centre, in the form of heavy traffic and parking restrictions.

77

As I go along the houses get very large indeed and quite interesting architecturally; number 17 seems to be a mixture of Tudorbethan and Arts and Crafts, an odd combination but still with a certain touch of class. [The houses on the most expensive roads in Ickenham are often designed in Essex scrap-dealer style.] To my right is King Edward's Road: "Private Road. Access Only", which is always a good indication of money so I can't resist a peek down it. Very pretty it is too, with an oak and other old trees.

Now I can turn up Sharp's Lane, which still is a lane at least in terms of width, and gives a nice feel of the countryside, Metro-land countryside. My first feeling is that if somebody revisited this estate eighty years on they probably wouldn't find that it had changed much, apart from the cars and the McDonald's debris which someone has kindly donated to it, and some infilling with newer houses. I come out at the top of the lane opposite the White Bear, with its lovely polar bear sign, at the former hamlet of Kingsend. To my left is The Orchard, now a Beefeater pub and restaurant, good value for pub snacks or full meals, though the service can be erratic. Regrettably it has lost the attractive sign that it had until recently. The remains of the original orchard are still in evidence and the apples look big and red and ready for scrumping, if I was about 45 years younger! It looks very open and wooded beyond and it is not difficult to imagine this establishment in its tea-room days, with the maids outside in their white pinafores as in a postcard I have, a focal point for country outings. As in Ickenham, if only you could block out the constant noise of the traffic, the scale and impact of which could hardly have been foreseen by the pedlars of the Metro-land dream.

I am walking now down the road called Kingsend back to the High Street. As I look back at The Orchard I can picture the orderly parties of well-scrubbed Sunday School children marching eagerly up the hill from the station towards it. On my left as I look back there are two cottages remaining from the original hamlet. Not much to comment on going down the hill though they are quite nice houses, one of them occupied by my dentist Mr [Coolfer] Katz. Dominating the view ahead is something that the children would not have seen on their way back to the station; a big block of flats, not particularly distinguished on the outside but a great improvement on the naff sixties offices from which they were converted.

On the High Street and walking back in the direction of the Manor Farm and the church I see an authentic suburban shopping street in a jumble of architectural styles but also, straight ahead on the horizon, the woods, again making it specifically Ruislip.

I have now crossed Eastcote Road by the church and am walking down St Martin's Approach with the car park on my left and am therefore entering the Pinn View Estate, heading towards the woods. These are the "detached Metro-land" houses that I saw earlier from behind and the fronts look even nicer, though some of the windows have been renewed rather unsympathetically. The trees along the verges are pretty if rather suburban. I come on to open space and cross the mighty River Pinn, in fact little more than a trickle, even smaller here than in Ickenham. To my right the prospect opens out to King's College Playing Fields [named for the original, Cambridge, land owner] and somewhere over there, although I cannot see it, is the Eastcote Hockey Club where my wife plays for the Ladies' [no women in hockey] Thirds. I am always impressed, if not by their results then by their spirit, in a team where the age gap between the oldest player and the youngest can be 35 years or more. It is all very pleasant in this Tory heartland of Ruislip Northwood and I am taking a detour to look at Broadwood Avenue, which I believe was actually carved out of the woods. Certainly there are some lovely old oak trees in the back gardens of the houses on the north side and I understand that the plan was to go on building into the woods. This was mercifully stopped, though as is usual in such cases with the fortunate result for the people in this road that they remain close to the woodland, perhaps a little too close for some tastes, in their large comfortable detached houses. A very pretty road – even today with the rubbish sacks piled up on the pavements for collection – and the woods look wonderful.

As I retrace my steps I note that this is a cul-de-sac as well, making it lovely and quiet [a boon in this area] with a pathway into the woods, which look very inviting. I have to resist the temptation but look at the notice by the path showing the wildlife to look out for, and marvel at the Metro-land houses on the very edge of the ancient forest. The promise is reality here for those who can afford it, and one of the houses even has stained-glass shields in the windows and heraldic devices in the brick work. Very baronial!

I am walking along Pinn Way now, with the "river" and fields on my left, and on my right more detached houses with leaded windows. Looking back I see houses that are effectively in the countryside with the Pinn on one side and the woods on the other. That is not taking account of how small the gap is *between* the houses! Somewhere along there are some more "modernist" houses, unusual round here, but I cannot see them. I cross the Eastcote Road into Manor Way and see some interesting cottage style houses, a relic of the garden city ideal. Some look a little like council houses but good ones, and some are very nice indeed. On checking at home in *The Buildings of England, London North West* [sic], 1991 edition, I find that this road was developed by the Ruislip Manor Cottage Society with "low rental housing for artisans, intended to serve the needs of the garden suburb planned for Ruislip-Northwood".

I am now on the Church Croft Estate and go into Midcroft Way, where the houses are smaller than those on the Pinn View Estate, some detached but a lot of semis. There is a variety of styles but a pleasant one, with plentiful trees and quite big gardens. Pretty much what Metro-land was intended to be. I turn down West Hatch Manor and on to the Windmill Estate. I look down Glenalla Road – a strange name, I wonder what the background was – a cul-de-sac, bungalows, the woods at the end. The housing now is a mixture of bungalows [surely the most wasteful way of building, albeit a boon to the elderly] and small detached houses, some chalet style. Reaching Windmill Hill I must look to the left to see the views that this estate was promised and, sure enough, straight down it I can see the green canopy of the woods, gradually shading into gold. There are the inevitable telecoms masts in there but all in all this estate looks pretty much as it was meant to. If I went in the other direction I would come to Ruislip Manor proper but I think that I will save that for later.

I walk back along Eastcote Road towards the old centre. It is a busy, noisy road and perhaps not ideal to live on for that reason, but some of the houses are interesting and again there are plenty of trees. I adjourn to the Six Bells for an early half. It is quite an old pub but with extensive children's play areas, making it busy in the summer.

Back to Warrender Way, on the Ruislip Manor Estate, very much given over to semis in a slightly "moderne" style with rounded windows at the front, the whole effect rather dominated by the Bishop Ramsey School at the end. It's a C of E school that used to take children from Christian families of all denominations in the area, but now brings in Anglican children from far afield and is effectively selective. How do they get away with it? Well, if the Prime Minister can do it .... My daughter says that in any case she would not have wanted to wear that drab [not her exact word] brown uniform.

I want to find the promised "preserved open space". Very much semi-dom here, though in Hawtrey Drive [named after one of the old land owners] some of them are quite big and with a number of detached houses. I am not quite sure what I expected of the open space [Warrender Park] but it is very nice indeed, with beautiful horse chestnut trees, poplars and oaks. The tennis courts are still here, looking rather run down, as they tend to these days [not enough Joan Hunter Dunns] but all in all this is a wonderful green oasis amongst the houses [particularly good obviously for the ones that back on to it] and another developer's promise kept, with views beyond the school to Park Wood and Northwood Hills.

I really feel that I am in Eastcote here [it is not very clear where the boundary is] but I am going to turn down Lime Grove to get down to Ruislip Manor proper. Myrtle Avenue has slightly more modest houses but is pretty, with a lot of preserved trees.

Now I am on the south side of the tracks but there is no immediate change of scenery, with plenty of trees amongst the bungalows. It begins to have a rather unadopted look with a jumble of architectural styles, but I am still in Eastcote and must get to Ruislip Manor.

I drive down Victoria Road, at this point the main Ruislip Manor shopping street, all rather run down, with quite a few shops boarded up, and turn into Shenley Avenue, which must have been part of the Ruislip Station Estate. The houses are still semis here and not bad, but it all feels rather hemmed in, packed close together and the road not very wide, and devoid of the country feel that prevails such a short distance away. I turn into Grosvenor Vale, which doesn't seem to go anywhere, like so many roads round here, still mostly small semis and with a sports ground at the end. But I note that some of them are terraced and I feel I am getting closer to the H.L. Bowers country. I turn down Torrington Road, one which actually goes somewhere, and I am in the true Ruislip Manor of bow-fronted terraces and not too many trees. As I turn right on to Victoria Road the spirits sink a little. I am heading away from

82

the woods and the higher ground. Even near the river it all looks a bit tatty.

On to South Ruislip, and tattier and tattier. I must take a look at Frazer Avenue, where I bought my first property [a "maisonette"]. I suppose that it is all right round here but perhaps it never recovered fully from its origins as a "squalid colony of huts and shacks". In central London areas like Islington can go down in the world and then rise again, but in the suburbs places that are down tend to stay down, perhaps because they are not worth reviving, though one might expect rising property prices at least to encourage people to invest in upkeep. It is all more run down than I remember it, though as I drive down Great Central Avenue I see the fields ahead of a still working [Priors] farm. Frazer Avenue looks more barren somehow than I remember and the appearance is not helped by the sacks of rubbish in one of the garages. The field at the end is very parched as I look across to the rather rough primary school, but the outlook is still open to the Western Avenue and towards Northolt, though I cannot believe that these fields ever justified the purple prose used for them in *London and Suburbs*. Down Deane Avenue, named after another former land-owning family and the pub used to be called the Deane Arms, though it has been renamed. The houses here still have the rather unharmonious, even unadopted, look of the frontier days and possibly the 1950s council flats on Station Approach replaced the hutments.

I head back to the northern uplands. To my left RAF Northolt [so-called] gives a nice open feeling but Ruislip Gardens is rather undistinguished, despite its Betjeman connection. Even the "preserved open spaces" look scrappy and scruffy.

Past the village I turn towards the Lido down Reservoir Road [a workaday name, why wasn't it renamed Lido View or some such?]. The sweetshop on the corner where we used to buy ice creams is boarded up [a bit sad], the chapel across the road is now a private house and there are more houses than there used to be. But I park the car and walk past the waterside pub that was rebuilt on the site of the old milk bar which was burnt down. The setting is wonderful but in my experience the service is terrible. The sun is on the water, there are plenty of swans with coots and other aquatic birds, and the woodland on the other side looks wonderful in its changing colours. The lake looks smaller than it used to and to some extent it really is, reflecting either the Great Drought of 2003 or that there is a leak, or possibly both. None the less it is still very beautiful and a fun place for children. The notice says that swimming is now forbidden [or was it always? We used to swim] but the railway still runs and the beach is sandy. The board also says that the reservoir was dug in 1811 and that in times of drought you can see the houses of the former hamlet of Park Hearn. Perhaps if I walked right round I could see it today but I do not have the time.

I stand at the entrance to Poor's Field, which as we have seen was originally given to the poor for grazing, and there are cows grazing on it now. I believe that this is for conservation reasons rather than poverty, except that all farmers claim to be poor. In any case it really is a piece of the country and it leads to Copse Wood.

Past the Six Bells on Duck's Hill Road I see a sign saying that the Old Workhouse is for sale [not sure that I have noticed that before]. There are fields on either side before the woods, which again look beautiful, with one or two cottages among the trees. I turn into the car park in the woods, though to describe them is beyond the scope of this book and the skill of this writer, but they are mostly ancient oaks with hornbeams underneath and used to be coppiced. A wonderful sight.

I go a bit further in the direction of Northwood and the woods open out to real countryside with farms, as well as the Holland & Holland shooting grounds. How traditional sounding! I am now reaching fat-cat Northwood, so will turn round in the quaintly named Fringewood Close.

Back along Breakspear Road I pass some nice old cottages hidden amongst the garages and builders' merchants and come to The Woodman pub, a nice reminder of the past and looking out on the woods and fields that remain today. Ruislip shows that you do not have to venture beyond Rickmansworth to experience the authentic Metro-land experience.

Further reading

A Short History of Ruislip The Ruislip Association, 1930

Ruislip-Northwood Through the Ages W.W. Druett, King and Hutchings, 1957

A History of Ruislip Laurence E. Morris, Ruislip, Northwood and Eastcote Local History Society, 2nd edition, 1980

The Goodliest Place in Middlesex Eileen M. Bowlt, Hillingdon Borough Libraries, 1989

A Quiet and Secluded Spot Colleen A. Cox, Ruislip, North-wood and Eastcote Local History Society, 1991

Bygone Ruislip and Uxbridge Dennis F. Edwards, Phillimore, 1995

Ruislip Past Eileen M. Bowlt, Historical Publications, 1994

Britain in Old Photographs, Ruislip, Ickenham & District Dennis F. Edwards, Sutton Publishing, 1996

The Archive Photographs Series, Around Ruislip Maria Newberry, Carolynne Cotton, Julie Ann Packham and Gwyn Jones, Chalford, 1996

4

Eastcote: the village that never was?

As far as I know, there is no reference to Eastcote in the
works of the Immortal Bard [or in Shakespeare for that
matter], a slight that it shares only with little Ickenham as far
as this book is concerned. When I was invited to a job inter-
view there I had to look it up on a map. Many of the source
books that I am using lump it in with Ruislip. The postal
address of my branch of HSBC in Field End Road, Eastcote,
is given as Pinner. Historically its name has been spelt many
different ways, so it may be felt to lack an identity. It does
not merit an entry in Weinreb and Hibbert's excellent *The
London Encyclopaedia*, while Ickenham gets eleven lines. It is
possible that it may not turn out to justify a chapter of its
own, but I see it as a distinct place with quite a variety of
scenery and architecture, some of it worth going to see. It
lacks the open spaces of Ickenham or Ruislip, but its original
core is better preserved than either of them.

Certainly, in earlier days there does not seem to have been
much to say about it, with Thorne telling us in 1876:

Eastcott, a large and pleasant hamlet, adjoins Pinner West End.
[HEL]

Foley does not say much more fourteen years later.

The bright little hamlet ...

... passing over the tiny bridge that spans a feeder of the River
Colne ... *[OLM]*

87

Walford in 1898 is one of those who include it with Ruislip, and cannot decide himself on the correct spelling, but he also shows that, some years earlier at least, its population had been larger than Ickenham's:

> ... *[in 1871]* of these *[Ruislip citizens]* ... no less than 500 belonged to Eastcot.

> *[Ruislip]* comprises several hamlets, which were doubtless manors in former times, and East-cote, Southcote and West-cot remain as local names.

At least Eastcote's name lives on into the 21st century, unlike its southern and western counterparts! It was fertile and had its share of gentry.

> The hamlet of Eastcote, sometimes called Ascot ... in the midst of a rich agricultural country. The mansion known as Eastcote House was formerly the seat of the Hawtrey family, who were once of great note in this parish .... .

> High Grove, another mansion in this locality, stands on a commanding site, and the grounds, which are about fifty acres in extent, are prettily laid out. *[GL]*

Just after the turn of the 20th century Firth looks at it with the eyes of a tourist, and likes what he sees.

> It is a delightful village, with strong claims to be considered among the most attractive in all Middlesex. It contains an unusual number of good houses, old homesteads with large barns and sweeping red-tiled roofs, and half-timbered cottages, many of which have been improved for modern dwellings. Through the village runs the Pin Brook. Eastcote House, on the south side of the stream, stands in spreading grounds on the site of the house where the Hawtreys lived, whose monuments are in Ruislip church. Opposite is Haydon Hall, a fine old-

fashioned house, to which large additions have been made. The country round is most pleasantly wooded, and abounds in footpaths. One fringes the edge of the beautiful Parkwood to Ruislip; another runs through it to the road at the head of Ruislip Reservoir. *[MF]*

I will be seeing later the extent to which this Arcadian vision survives, but his views at the time were certainly supported by Hope Moncrieff. The latter however makes similar dire warnings of the likely impact of the Met to those he did in the case of Ruislip:

One ramble of two or three hours to be suggested is by a chain of old-world villages, such as often surprise one in this populous county, as do quaint tumbledown cottages here and there preserved like flies in the amber of a spick-and-span suburb. But how long will these hamlets keep their rusticity, now that they are threaded by the Metropolitan branch to Uxbridge, not to speak of the new Great Central and Great Western joint line to Wycombe? Before the foul breath of London has blighted them, let my client, by one of two or three ways, make for Eastcote, a most rustic straggling of cottages a mile or two south-west from Pinner. When he has got to the end of this village on the road to Ruislip, a bridge on the right shows him where to take a field path along a brook, then under the edge of the large Park Wood, in which is set Ruislip Lake, another of those canal reservoirs that make such a fine show in Middlesex. *[MFH]*

Eastcote then seemed almost to slip off the map again, with even Jerrold, who waxed lyrical over Ruislip, only mentioning it in passing as an "attractive hamlet". But with the end of the Great War this was not a situation that *Metro-land* was going to allow to persist, pointing out that amidst the sleeping rustics some new developments had already taken place.

Eastcote ... *[stands]* ... in a countryside of hill and dale, and is all the better for that circumstance. It is a dainty little old hamlet, wandering back among the centuries, combined with some agreeably constructed modern residences and shops. In spite of these innovations, the whole district is pervaded with a farm-yard atmosphere, which the jaded town-dweller inhales with a sense of gratitude.

I am very happy to live opposite farm land, but none the less feel constrained to point out that a "farm-yard atmosphere" is not something one always "inhales with a sense of gratitude". The important point however is that further development was slow here as elsewhere in the immediate post-war period. The emphasis is on the attractions to trippers.

Eastcote possesses several ancestral mansions, such as Eastcote Hall and Haydon Hall; it is likewise a popular holiday resort, with catering facilities sufficient for the needs of several thousands at a time. The neighbouring lake or reservoir – a spacious sheet of transparent water – affords a pleasing contrast to the surrounding landscape, and is provided with ample boating facilities.

The "neighbouring" lake being claimed as an Eastcote asset is of course the Ruislip one, but Eastcote has its own attractions:

The Pavilion: Specially designed and arranged for School and other Parties. Extensive accommodation. Large playing fields.

Ship Inn and Pavilion: Beautiful Tea Gardens. Parties catered for. Concerts and Dances every Wednesday.

Ashtree Tea Gardens: Adjoining Post Office. High-class Luncheons, Dinners, Teas etc. Small parties catered for.

There is little mention of housing development around Eastcote itself:

34 houses erected by the local council; further 55 contemplated; 70 privately contracted for.

But interestingly Ruislip Manor is covered in the Eastcote section. [Identity again!]

A little further on we come to Ruislip Manor, which though served by the Metropolitan Railway, has not yet arrived at the dignity of a station, but only a "Halt". Here is situated the Ruislip Manor Estate, designed to be laid out as a Garden City. *[ML 1921]*

In the 1928 edition of *Metro-land* there is mention of development but a strong emphasis still on the attractions for tourists.

Eastcote is one of the most charming villages in Middlesex. Certainly on this side of the County it is without a rival.

But there is a north/south divide here as in Ruislip and even this most enthusiastic of publications has little positive to say about the wrong [south] side of the tracks.

The broad plain from the station towards Northolt is rather devoid of interest, but the hamlet of Eastcote lies on the other side of the railway, strung out along the high road borders the Pin rivulet and the delightful lanes which run up towards the gentle eminence of Haste Hill, in the direction of Northwood.

There are some houses of age and distinction here, notably Eastcote Hall and Haydon Hall, standing in their own grounds, but the real charm of the place consists in the old farm houses, with their red-tiled barns, a few half-timbered dwellings and a number of picturesque cottages, with gardens where the flowers grow in gay profusion.

More specific attractions are fewer, unless the visitor tramps as far as the Lido, though by this time we are told "The Pavilion" seats "4000 under cover". A major enterprise indeed.

Near the station are several sports grounds and boating may be had on the neighbouring lake .... .

References to building are still concentrated on Ruislip Manor, though there is other activity.

A little further on is the station which serves the Ruislip Manor Estate, now being laid out as a Garden City. Other building companies are also busy in the neighbourhood.

And under "The Estates" [Homes section] we find:

Eastcote Hill Estate: very fine Sites ... are offered, adjoining Station and shopping centre, for erection of detached or semi-detached Houses and Bungalows .... . Land reserved for Tennis Courts. Houses now ready from £995 Freehold and £25 secures possession. [ML 1928]

Not only houses but the amenities to go with them, including a promise of the essential tennis courts, and by 1932 *Metroland* is describing a different place. The Pavilion still advertises its "ample amusements" but the tide of houses is lapping against it [to use the sort of expression that was favoured by inter-war writers]. Village Eastcote is almost past tense. A new Eastcote is rising fast in the south.

92

Eastcote has always been regarded as one of the most attractive villages on this side of the county of Middlesex. Old Eastcote, that is to say, for a new is rapidly rising around the station.

Four hundred houses have been built within a short period and preparations have been made for another two thousand. What was ten years ago the poplar-lined country lane between the station and Eastcote is now becoming a line of shops.

The old name of this portion of Eastcote was Fieldend, and there seems a tendency to retain it in connection with the new suburb, whose population now equals that of Eastcote proper.

A short way beyond Eastcote on the railway is the station that serves the Ruislip Manor Estate, now being laid out as a Garden City. Both here and on the Ruislip Manor Garden Estate there is a steady demand for good houses at a reasonable price and ample provision is made to meet it. *[ML 1932]*

On the "old" Eastcote Hill Estate the "prices from" has dropped by £20 to £975 and the land is still "reserved" for tennis courts, suggesting that they remain a promise rather than a reality! There is also mention of "extensive housing development on Eastcote Hill Estate and in locality by W.A. Telling Ltd. and T.F. Nash Ltd., etc".

Outside the pages of *Metro-land*, references to Eastcote are again brief, though the views of Martin S. Briggs on the new development are covered in the Ruislip chapter. He does comment on the area of the old village:

Most of the picturesque banks of the little River Pin are protected ... though one of the "grid" pylons has been placed plumb in the middle of a charming meadow by the Pin at Eastcote. *[MON]*

Clunn confines himself to referring to

> ... the new suburb of Eastcote ... *[TFL]*

but Pevsner reassures us that not all has been lost:

> ... many good farmhouses and outbuildings survive, scattered
> amid modern domestic development. *[BEM]*

Overall I have been surprised by how little the coverage was of
Eastcote over the years, not in comparison with Ruislip but
with Ickenham. I will look for clues as to why this might be
the case as I do my walkabout.

I visit Eastcote on a sunny day at the end of October, with
the trees looking lovely as the leaves come down. According
to the *Daily Mail* this morning, the autumn of 2003 is one of
the best ever and in Eastcote you can believe it. I have come
here from the Northwood Hills direction, down Joel Street
and passing preserved farmland on my left, and I have
stopped in what were the grounds of Haydon Hall, looking
across to the pavilion of the Eastcote Cricket Club. It is not
particularly distinguished, a fairly modern prefabricated
wooden job, but the overall scene is very pretty. There is a
pub over the other side called The Woodman, the name as in
the case of the one at Ruislip a memory of past local industry.
It looks inviting, even at this early hour, and behind it I can
see houses nestling among the trees. There is a house on the
north side, detached, substantial, Tudorbethan, with a
beautiful view across the park, in which are dotted some fine
old oaks and elms. In the corner a rather distinguished-
looking Georgian farmhouse with a small stable and a
paddock behind it, really feeling like the countryside. And just
ahead is the country pub with the rather strange name of The
Case is Altered, which I believe is something to do with the
Peninsular War, as used to be represented on its sign, but I
find that the picture has now almost disappeared. I hope that
they have it redone, because the current trend of chains such

as Ember Inns to replace distinctive pub signs with their boring corporate logos is almost [but not quite] as depressing as the parallel trend for pubs themselves to be converted to McDonald's, or even to executive housing. I spent many a happy Friday evening in this establishment when I worked in the area, our crowd [and this was part of the problem] being rather unpopular with an elderly local who we called Mr O Christ, because of what he used to say when we arrived and he left. To my left as I look at the pub is a very nice half-timbered house with beautifully carved posts round the front door and even some of the brickwork is embossed. A little notice on it says Haydon Lodge *c*.1880. A later check in Pevsner reminds me not only that this lodge is "a typical example of George and Peto's Dutch revival" but also that fifty years ago Haydon Hall itself was still standing ["a sound late C17 brick house"].

Standing on the bridge over the Pinn I note that the river here is still moving rather slowly, despite the fact that we have finally had some rain recently. There are some beautiful overhanging trees, but as usual yobs have thrown their rubbish here, where "Every prospect pleases and only man is vile". As I walk along the open space near the river I can see the pub to my left and some old houses amongst the trees. A sign board by the river is headed, surprisingly, "Celandine Route, a walk of twelve miles along the River Pinn from Pinner to the Grand Union canal at Cowley through green spaces, conservation areas and wildlife havens". Well, I am not going to have time to do this today but it is worth bearing in mind for another occasion. There is a nice little footbridge [a real Poohsticks job] across to what were the grounds of Eastcote House. Along the south side of the river I can see plenty of housing development, but to the north is the green space I am walking along and a wonderful wooden farmhouse. In fact it seems to be more than one house and at the end are offices for Portcullis Computer Security Ltd. There is a little close of 1970s flat-roofed houses here but beyond it is the paddock I mentioned previously. One at least of the buildings is separate; it is called Grange Cottage, built in the wooden Middlesex style. The next house is called The Old Shooting Box and looks a genuine enough reminder of the rural past. There is some really distinguished housing here, looking snug amongst the trees with a prospect across the open space to the river, and only the busy, noisy road to spoil the idyll. As I walk further along there is a variety of housing, some of it quite expensive looking, mostly detached but a little less distinguished and distinctive than at the beginning, where it was comforting to find that a lot of the old farmhouses mentioned in the books are still there today. Ickenham possesses a number of working farms but in a way the past is more evident here, and certainly more evident than in Ruislip outside the Manor Farm area, which itself is slightly museum-like.

I branch off to the left up Catlins Lane, where the houses definitely look like some of the first to be built once Eastcote started to develop, with an Edwardian appearance, some detached and some semis but all substantial, with big mature-looking hedges as befits a development 100 or so years old. I realise that I am approaching the Cuckoo Hill area. As I go on up it all feels very nice. I come to some fairly modern [1990s?] houses, which I imagine caused some controversy when they were built, and then a field at the top, with what looks an old iron farm gate in front of it. All in all a pleasant "suburban countryside" feel. As I walk back I try to get a view of the housing to the south but it is not very easy due to the trees, which have not yet lost most of their leaves.

I am now going to turn right along Cheney Street and back over the Pinn, to look at another part of Eastcote that was developed pre WW1, after the opening of the Met station but quite a step from it. There are one or two quite big houses at this end, one with big iron gates and some sort of security

The romance of the railway: who needs Switzerland?

Lucerne/Mount Pilatus 1900

Harrow-on-the-Hill 1913.
And only minutes from the city

Metro-land, bible of the tripper and the house buyer

Poster for the 1930 edition
© TfL Reproduced courtesy of London's Transport Museum

The promise of the Barn Hill Estate (Advertisement in the 1928 edition)

BARN HILL ESTATE WEMBLEY PARK

A typical 4-bedroom Haymills House. Type "N". Price £1300. Ground Rent £9.

280 feet above Sea Level
Situated on the Southern and Western slopes of Barn Hill in the health-giving air of the open country, Barn Hill Estate has rapidly developed into one of the most attractive and convenient residential estates in N.W. London. More than 1,000 detached houses containing 3, 4 or 5 bedrooms are being built.

44 acres have been purchased by the Wembley Council for a Public Park. Every house will have a good garden back and front and space for a garage. Shops are already open on the estate. Golf and Tennis Clubs are within easy reach.

10 minutes from Baker Street
Wembley Park and Preston Road stations (Metro, Rly.) adjoin the Estate. The new arterial road affords motorists direct communication with London and all parts of the country.
Rates 5/- in the £ for half-year. Main drainage. Colne Valley Company's water.

Visit Barn Hill Estate
and inspect the houses in course of construction. The Estate Office is 280 yds. from Wembley Park Stn. (turn left) and representatives are in constant attendance, including Saturdays and Sundays.

Gas and Electric light to all rooms. Space for Garage included in purchase price. Interior decorations finished to purchaser's choice.
Prices from **£1,175 to £2,000**
(Leasehold and Freehold).
Liberal advances by Cheshunt Bdg. Scy.

Write or 'phone for Booklet "C" giving particulars, plans and prices of the various types of Houses being erected, and other most useful information. Free on request.

HAYMILLS, LTD
1, GRAND PARADE
Forty Lane, Wembley Park
Telephone: Wembley 1736.

HAYMILLS HOUSES

SAY YOU SAW IT IN "METRO-LAND."

Page 103

"Wonderful Wembley"

A promise kept on Barn Hill

© Greg Ward

King Edward VII Park, outlook towards Harrow Hill

© Greg Ward

Rural Ickenham

From the north west

From the south east

"Ruislip for the quiet English countryside"

eace in north Ruislip

he mighty River Pinn

Suburban pride: the Eastcote Park Estate

Entrance

Authentic Metro-land

Aspects of Greater Harrow

Woodcock Hill, Northwick Park

Timeless scene, Headstone Manor Park

Leafy Pinner

Pinner Park

"Artisans' Dwellings", Albury Drive

system, before I come to what I imagine is the start of the development I am looking for – large houses looking much as they were intended to and very attractive, even allowing for the fact that I am seeing everything on a perfect day. This is suburbia as it should be; a variety of houses, including some 1970s-style ones with huge picture windows, like living in a goldfish bowl, then a very substantial Tudorbethan house at least 100 years old I should think, wide verges and plenty of trees. At the southern end are what I assume to be some of the early houses to be built: substantial and detached, if rather close together.

Now into Bridle Road [pleasantly rural name] and I am confronted with a rather mysterious building called Missouri Court, owned by the London Borough of Hillingdon and consisting of little flats. An old folks home, perhaps? The houses along here include older-style Tudorbethan semis, which fit quite well with Eastcote's remaining genuinely old houses and cottages, though the road itself is wider than the High Road and seems even noisier. St Lawrence's Church is in a distinctive inter-war style. [I look it up in Pevsner when I get home. He spells it wrongly and says that it is 1932–3 by Sir William Nicholson; "a pleasant interior with Tuscan columns, wide arches and wagon roof".] I notice that the Vicar is the Rev. David Coleman and wonder how often he shows his class. More relevantly I wonder if the fact that Eastcote did not have its own parish church was one of the factors helping to cause its relative anonymity.

Something of interest along here is an elaborate wrought-iron sign with pictures of trees on it and doves on the top saying "Eastcote Park Estate 1937–1997". I have to take a look and find an attractive estate of detached houses and semis, with plenty of trees to hand and in the distance, and it becomes quite quiet as I walk further, seeming to be another case of an idyll as advertised. The residents obviously think so as they proudly proclaim their estate 60 years on. Well, it was

97

[I am told by Edwards] developed by Comben and Wakeling, the builders of my childhood home in Wembley.

I turn into the delightfully named Pamela Gardens, which seems to contain houses of every known suburban style: Tudorbethan, Dutch gable, Suntrap, but they blend to good effect. There is certainly no monotony! [Pamela, I subsequently find, was the daughter of a member of the Wakeling family.]

I am now in Field End Road, again a pleasantly countrified name, commemorating as we have seen the original hamlet to the south, though at this end it was one of the first places that was subject to development in the mid 19th century. One example still has a monkey-puzzle tree in its garden. There is some pleasant open space as well, with the remaining grounds of the former Eastcote House, which I see was not demolished until the 1960s. Pevsner certainly described it in 1951: "an insignificant whitewashed Georgian exterior covers some C16 and C17 remains inside". Have threats to historic buildings now ended? Not so, if you look at the plans for Heathrow T5 and Government efforts to undermine environmental and heritage watchdogs.

A quick look along the High Road, with the house numbering starting as 1, 2 etc. on some rather undistinguished properties, but they are succeeded on the left by a pretty half-timbered cottage with a car wash and valeting centre next to it which looks at least pre-war, though presumably not with that function. I am walking in the direction of the old Black Horse pub but have to pass a totally dreary and naff 1960s shopping parade. Who perpetrated this horror? But across the road it is pleasantly green with another sign for the Celandine Route, reminding me that "in 1908 the Olympic Marathon runners passed through Eastcote village. The mediaeval Old Barn had already been in use for several centuries, another long running achievement" [ho! ho!]. It also says that Haydon Hall was demolished in 1967. There are some nice old cottages opposite

98

the pub, which seems to be closed for refurbishment. I hope that it is refurbishment and not for turning into another McDonald's. [At the time of preparing this book for publication I am pleased to report that the Black Horse has reopened, though I have not tried it yet.] Walking back I notice that the car wash is called Grime Stoppers [very good]. More to the point, I believe that the smithy stood where the Gulf service station is now across the road, and this was certainly the heart of the old village.

On Field End Road I notice an old gatepost at the entrance to the Eastcote House grounds and also some nice cottages, including the one with the monkey-puzzle tree. Eastcote Methodist Church is on the left, in a typical inter-war Nonconformist style. Just past it is Park Farm Close and the farmhouse is still there, whitewashed at one end, wood-clad at the other and a nice cottagey garden. It is surrounded by semis. There's a sign here to Retreat Cottage, which is quaintly half-timbered but with a 1970s terrace behind it. I get into conversation with [I assume] the owner of the cottage who was asking what I was up to. We get off on the wrong foot, but he explains that they have had a lot of trouble recently, including an arson attack on an empty house down the lane, and he ends up saying that he would buy this book if it ever came out! I pass the St Thomas More RC Church, a 1970s job, and am interested to note as I head towards the station the fingerpost in the road saying "Eastcote half a mile", removing all doubt as to where the centre is now. The Tudor Lodge Hotel looks nice, from the outside anyway, and at least in part genuinely old.

I am now arriving at an unmistakeable parade of inter-war shops that was dumped on the sleeping countryside, though there is a nice old barn, refurbished and functioning as offices for the City Partnership firm of solicitors. That is what I like to see, good use being made of old buildings. There is actually quite an extensive range of [albeit small] shops here, it is just the architectural effect that is so depressing. Not run down and dirty like Wembley, but dreary and jumbled, and in an indescribable mishmash of styles. Next I come to Morford Way, which was part of the Telling development on the Eastcote End Park Estate, and I venture down it for a look at what one might call "Middle Eastcote". It is actually quite pleasant, the houses mostly detached, but the road is narrow, giving much less feeling of space than in some I was looking at earlier. In Morford Close there are some bungalows and semis, mostly with quite decent lengths of garden, but there is a feeling of being enclosed by other houses. Into Hawthorn Way and heading for Lime Grove there are houses built on plots sold by British Freehold Investments, which were a cause of concern because of the absence of planning. Looking at it now and ignoring the traffic, it does not look particularly distinguished but nor does it seem to vindicate the direr forebodings. Arriving at Eastcote station, I can see the sundry, nondescript, small office blocks just to the south of the line, in one of which, Audit House, I used to work, though it has been poshed up a bit since.

Walking back I am taking a peek at some of the housing to the east of Field End Road, starting by looking down North View, which appears to offer a prospect of endless semis, quite close together. I then stroll down Abbotsbury Gardens, decent suburban semis in Tudorbethan style, mostly well looked after, but I can see from the map that this is quite a long road and there are quite a lot of them. There are trees, but again the road is narrow with cars parked on either side and it is all rather hemmed in. A look down Deane Court Road, which seems slightly more open, but the same feelings apply. Perfectly good houses but too many of them and going on too long a way. You need quite a lot of imagination to feel that you are anywhere close to the countryside here.

As I walk back north, once I am past the shops everything seems to open out again and become greener and more interesting. Is it all about money? Perhaps money plus the shape of the landscape to start with, though these were connected anyway, as suggested by some of the extracts.

I stop for a pint and a sandwich at The Case is Altered and it is what a village local should be. A blazing fire, regulars with their own tankards, even a man bringing a huge greyhound in. You don't often see dogs in pubs these days. There is a golf match coming up and there are games available to play in the pub. All just as it should be, and perhaps helping to explain why they used to resent being invaded by a noisy horde of outsiders on a Friday night all those years ago.

The sun has gone in during my lunch and the wind has got up, so it is lucky that I have done most of my planned walking and am doing my remaining visits by car. First up Fore Street, one of Eastcote's old streets, with some nice old cottages and quite a lot of local authority development, mostly pleasant and including some cottage-style ones from before WW1. It becomes quite open on the left with riding stables and a nursery alongside Park Wood.

Back in the car I head south of the tracks and park opposite the Cavendish Function Room, which is close to the site of the old Pavilion and is in front of sports grounds where we used to play rather informal cricket matches against clients. There are lots of smallish semis backing on to it but looking rather close together, and I drive round to look at the fronts of them in Ferncroft Avenue. The houses are not bad, but there are too many of them and often with the front gardens paved over for cars to park on, despite which the road is full of parked cars. Then into Pavilion Way, so I know that I am close to what was the heart of day-tripper Eastcote, though the attractions are no longer very evident. When I reach Whitby Road I realise that I am close to Ruislip Manor so I turn and come out at a suburban roadhouse now calling itself Venue 5, Bar, Restaurant and

101

Banqueting, but when I worked round here it was called the Clay Pigeon, a connection with earlier days. The landlord was as mean as hell, but I remember him providing drinks on the house for the skiving market researchers who had been watching Bob Willis take 8 for 43 to finish off the Australians in the 1981 Headingley [Botham's] Test. Those were the days! There is quite a lot of open space here but on the whole as one heads towards Northolt it becomes less attractive. As I have mentioned previously, the north/south divide favours the north round here, but I come away believing that all in all there are worse places to live than Eastcote, and many with fewer traces of the rural past.

Further reading

In keeping with the overall picture, some [though not all] of these titles are duplicated from the Ruislip chapter.

Ruislip-Northwood Through the Ages W.W. Druett, King and Hutchings, 1957

The History of Eastcote, Middlesex W.A.G. Kemp, The Author, 1963

Eastcote, From Village to Suburb Ron Edwards, Hillingdon Borough Libraries, 1987

The Goodliest Place in Middlesex Eileen M. Bowlt, Hillingdon Borough Libraries, 1989

A Quiet and Secluded Spot Colleen A. Cox, Ruislip, Northwood and Eastcote Local History Society, 1991

Bygone Ruislip and Uxbridge Dennis F. Edwards, Phillimore, 1995

Ruislip Past Eileen M. Boult, Historical Publications, 1994

Britain in Old Photographs, Ruislip, Ickenham & District Dennis F. Edwards, Sutton Publishing, 1996

The Archive Photographs Series, Around Ruislip Maria Newbery, Carolynne Cotton, Julie Ann Packham and Gwyn Jones, Chalford, 1996

5

"... upward to the heights of Harrow Hill"

Of the places covered in this book, Harrow is by far the most prominent in every way. This is literally true, indicated by the fact that I can see the spire of St Mary's as I inexpertly thump my keyboard, six miles away in Ickenham. It is a towering height in the setting of a mostly flat county. But it is also true in another sense: Eastcote is a name on a tube map, Harrow is known round the world. This is of course mainly to do with the school and/or Byron and the Hill, though the prospect from the latter shows the extent of the spread of bricks and mortar, as well as the occasional gaps, resulting from 20th-century development. Harrow is also, depending on how you define it, big, and covers a variety of villages and settlements.

Thorne in 1876 starts at the obvious place:

Harrow on the Hill, famous for its church, its hill, and the pro-spects from it, and above all its school .... .

Harrow Hill rises, abrupt and isolated, some 200 ft. from the plain ... . With the spire of the church which crowns its summit ... Harrow Hill is a conspicuous, and, from its form, a pleasing feature in the landscape for many miles on every side, but especially S. and W.

We have here a town when the other places featured in this book were only villages, or even hamlets. But a town that owes much to the school.

The town ... occupies the crest and follows the slopes of the hill. The school dominates and colours it, and has seized on the best positions. As a rule the shops are small, but those which provide for the school, and the many affluent families the school has led to settle around it, are of course exceptions. Besides the school buildings, there are many masters' houses sufficiently spacious to receive boarders, and many good private residences, the former invariably and the latter mostly, modern gothic, of a kind to harmonise with the school buildings, together giving to the town a thoroughly distinctive character – a character that every visitor feels is at once unique and appropriate .... .

It is a town with modern amenities:

It has ... Gas and Waterworks, ... Workmen's Hall, a Public Hall and Assembly Room, built in 1874, and a Cottage Hospital, for which a neat building was erected opposite the cricket field in the Roxeth Road in 1872.

surrounded by beautiful countryside:

The prospect as seen from *["Byron's Tomb"]* ... is really very fine, especially on a clear summer's evening. It reaches W. and S.W. across Roxeth Common, and a broad expanse of level, but richly wooded and cultivated scenery .... .

but already benefiting or suffering from new development, for good:

Roxeth ... may fairly be reckoned a part of Harrow, being joined to it by the many new buildings; but it was formerly an outlying hamlet ... It has ... some good modern residences.

or ill:

106

Greenhill ... has the look of a suburban railway growth and is not attractive.

But more salubrious parts are close by:

Harrow Weald is the broad level tract N. of Harrow, extending from Harrow Station to Stanmore. Of old ... a wild woodland, it has long been enclosed and cultivated; but it still has a good deal of timber; and the walk across it to Stanmore Common is very pleasant. The hamlet of Harrow Weald ... has little to attract or interest the stranger, but there are some good farmhouses and private residences. *[HEL]*

Harrow is well known for Byron and the associated views, but rather unjustifiably in the opinion of Foley:

We confess to a feeling that the view from Harrow Churchyard has been overrated. ... we cannot help fancying that if had not been Lord Byron's habit as a boy to lie full length on a certain tomb and gaze at the landscape, very much less rapture would have been expressed. It might even be thought that the level tract of country stretched at our feet was somewhat tame and monotonous. ... But from the tower we overlook the surrounding trees and buildings, and are able fully to appreciate the isolated character of Harrow Hill. ... Northwards ... the ... country is very beautiful. In the memory of the older inhabitants the land about here was a succession of yellow cornfields; now we see it all under grass, Harrow rising like a bold headland from a vivid sea of verdure.

The flat countryside has evolved from corn to grass and, as we have seen, the step from grass to bricks is already starting. Foley also introduces us to the town, which is blessed with open space close by:

Passing down the High Street we come to a wide open space in the centre of the town. To our right is the King's Head Hotel and opposite is the public hall. A turning just beyond the latter brings us to Harrow Park, a retired spot where we may enjoy visions of woody slopes, or a bright expanse of green meadows stretching away towards Hampstead and Highgate.

Despite the development already noted, Roxeth and its immediate vicinity are still of interest to readers of a book entitled *Our Lanes and Meadowpaths*.

To the right of the High Street, a little south-east of the church, is the district of Roxeth, formerly an outlying hamlet, but now joined to Harrow. ... There are several picturesque buildings still to be found, and beyond the village the lime-washed farm-steads and cottages have a very happy look. From Roxeth a charming little green lane leads to Pinner village, in springtime passing between fragrant hedges of hawthorn the greater part of the way.

There are rural attractions to south as well, in the charming and sparsely inhabited Vale of Middlesex.

Southwards from Harrow there stretches a pleasant and exten-sive valley, known as the Vale of Middlesex, and remarkable as containing only two or three habitations in the space of several square miles. ... Throughout the vale the Grand Junction Canal traces its course; and the various branches and feeders of the River Brent wander listlessly about it.

I have to confess that, until embarking on this book, I had no idea that there was or ever had been a Vale of Middlesex, embracing "interesting little villages" such as Northolt, Green-ford, Perivale and West Twyford.

> ... this charmingly rural neighbourhood to the south of Harrow ... succession of most interesting little villages ... each placed amid gentle woodland scenery, girt round with the brightest of green meadows, behind which rises the long and leafy flank of Harrow Hill.

There is plenty of room to stretch the legs to the north as well:

> Northward ... there are large unenclosed stretches of waste lands while the numerous large parks, such as Bentley Priory, Weald Park, Stanmore Park and Belmont, with the smaller estates of Woodlands and the Hermitage, enclose a considerable amount of timber and many ancient trees.

Not forgetting Headstone Manor, former country residence of the Archbishops of Canterbury where it is sometimes claimed that Becket stayed, in its splendid rural isolation.

> Between towering hedgerows overrun with huge tangled masses of bramble, where the rich, ripe fruit hangs in clusters, we pass along a broad green approach to the ancient site; and a bend soon reveals to us two long lines of weatherworn red roofs upon which the orange-coloured lichens have long held sway, and between an old orchard and a group of fine new haystacks we reach an angle of the ancient moat which still surrounds the substantial-looking dwelling-house and gardens. ... Tall poplars, willows, elms and a few yews in the gardens, show a greater variety of tree growth than we find round an ordinary Middlesex farmhouse. We cross the farmyard between two rare old barns of enormous length, and beyond these we catch glimpses of another larger orchard, where amid the shadows cast by the gnarled old trees, the afternoon sun is forming brilliant patches of golden turf. [OLM]

Walford mentions another vale, this time of Harrow, but

again embracing a fairly rural locality, with the bonus of hunting.

> The broad vale of Harrow, which stretches from the foot of the hill to Edgware and Stanmore in the north-east, and to Uxbridge and Hayes in the south-west ... .The roads are muddy and miry in winter ... .The district, however, smiles sweetly in early June, and has its attractions for the hunter in the winter season.

> Outside the churchyard, on the western slope of the hill, a terrace has been formed with seats for visitors. The view from this spot is very extensive, embracing as it does the green and level expanse of western Middlesex ....

He confirms that Harrow is a modern, and growing, town:

> In 1891 the number of inhabited houses was 2,526, the population numbering some 12,988 souls; but such has been the additional advantage offered of late years by railway communication with the metropolis ... that the number of inhabitants is increasing with great rapidity. The town, too, possesses its Fire Brigade, its Literary Institution, Assembly Rooms and District Council offices. The Public Hall is a large building of "Elizabethan" design, capable of holding upwards of 600 persons; it was erected in 1877 by a limited liability company. There is also a Cottage Hospital, which was erected in 1872 ... Harrow also has its gas and waterworks, its recreation ground, and its weekly "Gazette".

But with rural delights close by for the tripper:

> Notwithstanding the gradual extension of London, and the speed with which most of the outlying villages are being connected one with another in all directions, there are still left a

110

few fields and hedgerows to which the cockney holidaymakers can partake themselves.

... Harrow Hill rises abrupt and isolated. Seen from this the elevating country for miles around has the appearance of an almost level plain.

But he is not in agreement with Foley about the extent of the transition in agriculture from corn to grass:

This surrounding land is mostly under cultivation for either corn or grass; indeed the land between Harrow and Heston ... still bears an excellent reputation for its corn, as it did in the time of "Good Queen Bess".

Walford concludes on a suburban note:

Between the town and the railway station, at the foot of the hill to the north, is Greenhill, a small cluster of villas and houses of modern growth. *[GL]*

In 1906 Firth also is concerned with suburban development and is for the most part not enamoured of it.

Harrow-on-the-Hill ... is one of the most picturesquely situated places in Middlesex .... . The amenities and beauty of Harrow have suffered very considerably of late years owing to the improved communication between it and London. By the station, at the northern foot of the hill, a much inferior Harrow is spreading rapidly, and South Harrow again can only be described as a poor suburb.

He gives credit where credit is due, though not commenting on the fact that those concerned, particularly from the school, had money and influence to back up their nimbyism.

The Harrow Park side, looking towards Sudbury and Wembley, is still happily unspoilt, and successful efforts have been made to preserve the slopes of the hill below the church.

But development to the north seems even more depressing than that to the south.

The northern suburb of Harrow, beyond the Metropolitan Railway Station on the road to Stanmore is called Greenhill, and has a good new stone church [St John's] at the fork of the roads. Greenhill ... straggles on to the Harrow and Wealdstone Station of the London and North-Western Railway, around which another very commonplace township, that of Wealdstone, is rapidly rising, throwing out branches right and left ... . Wealdstone now extends, almost without a break in the houses, to the southern portion of Harrow Weald, which is gradually sharing the same fate. The old hamlet is being swallowed by the new cottages and small villas.

Fortunately, a little further north again money plays its role in blocking development.

Harrow Weald lies at the foot of rising ground, and the northern part of it retains all its old picturesque-ness, thanks to the few large houses with well wooded grounds which cover most of this part of the parish. ... The Common ... stretches westward from the inn ... affording splendid views toward Harrow.

But Headstone Manor is losing its seclusion.

Headstone Manor lies in the fields between Wealdstone and Pinner. Until recent years it was quite remote from any other habitation; now Harrow is fast extending out in its direction.
[MF]

112

Hope Moncrieff a year later is positive about development, as long as it is for the benefit of the better sort of person:

> But as day-boys are admitted *[to the school]* as well as boarders in the masters' houses, families of the better class have been brought to settle here, to the prospering of Harrow, now expanded with a population of over 10,000, spread out in smart streets and lines of villas that run into once outlying hamlets.

> The meadows round the hill are traversed by footways, some of them, indeed, overlaid by new roads; but there still run many pleasant pathways through the fields .... *[MFH]*

This positive note is echoed by Mrs Bell in the same year:

> From the loftier Highwood Hill, close to Mill Hill, a noble view is obtained of the beautiful Harrow Weald, that stretches away in a north-westerly direction to Harrow-on-the Hill, and is dotted with picturesque villages and hamlets, some of which are still unspoiled by the invasion of the builder. *[SGC]*

Where to Live Round London highlights The Headstone Estate specifically:

> The beauty of its position and its healthiness, and its convenience of access from town ... have served to make Harrow much esteemed as a place of residence. The Headstone Estate is available for residential purposes.

This estate was to the south of the Manor, but in the vanguard of the developments threatening its seclusion. According to the advertisement for it, there were attractions both to the wallet and the lungs, though it is not altogether clear on what the "high" claim was based:

> Enjoys lower rates than any other part of the Town. High and

113

healthy. Adjoins the Harrow Recreation Grounds, with the advantage of Private Entrance. Capital sites and houses to be sold or let. Apply to Clarke & co., The Harrow Estate Offices ... *[WTL]*

For once Jerrold has little to say and that very mixed:

... Harrow, with its ever growing modern additions, is in parts taking on some of the unloveliness of suburbia .... Its rows of villas, large and small, are eating into the pastures, yet also in parts it remains unspoiled .... *[HBI]*

In 1921 *Metro-land* can claim Harrow as its own, and even make its trains sound poetic:

... a pleasant dwelling place for City business men, who from their office reach their homes in about half-an-hour – from Baker Street, fifteen minutes.

The red brick Elizabethan [*well, some of them*] buildings of the School crown the Hill which, at an altitude of 400 feet, dominates the surrounding landscape, which is steadily growing into a great, detached London residential suburb. The electric trains that bind Harrow to the Metropolis are rarely at rest.

Under "Other Housing Developments in Metro-land", there is mention of the Council building a number of houses on the Honeybun [!] Estate and in Bessborough Road, but the only private building mentioned is on the Glebe Estate:

The Glebe Estate, Harrow: Semi-detached Brick-Built Villas on this Estate, ideally situated within 3 minutes of North Harrow Station.

Houses can be erected on this estate to Clients' or their Architects' design if required. A. Cutler, Builder. *[ML 1921]*

Note the flexibility to have an architect design one for you!
Many of the developers themselves were [in]famous for not
using architects.

By 1928 *Metro-land* can say:

> There are two Harrows. One is the Harrow of the Plain, which
> of late years has grown very fast, northward towards Weald-
> stone and the high ground of Harrow Weald, and westward
> and southward towards Pinner and Roxeth. The other is
> Harrow-on-the Hill, crowned nobly by the church and the
> buildings of the famous school, with a high road along the
> windy ridge which still retains many traces of its village days.
> ... The *[school]* cricket fields lie on the lower slopes of the hill
> towards Roxeth, and the pleasant slopes looking towards
> London were saved by subscription among friends of the
> school to save them from the advancing tide of bricks and
> mortar.

Metro-land somehow seems to distance itself from the forces
responsible for this advancing tide! But elsewhere it continues
to seek opportunities to create new season ticket holders.

> At Harrow the electric line to Uxbridge branches off. The first
> halt is at West Harrow, where a considerable suburb has
> sprung up, and the next at Rayner's Lane, which still awaits
> development.

But not for long! Progress will soon be here, as at Headstone
Manor.

> ... the ancient moated Headstone Farm, lying between Pinner
> and Harrow .... Till quite recently it retained its old seclusion.
> The moat is still intact and supplied with running water.

Under "Other Housing Developments" there is mention of:

Extensive private building operations at both West Harrow and North Harrow .... Council are building 154 houses in Eastcote Lane.

The ads show plenty of competition at North Harrow between Reid and Cutler, both with offerings at the lower end of the price range.

Reid Houses, North Harrow Station: [*prices £750–£1,600*]

North Harrow Estates [Cutlers Ltd.]: semi-detached Brick-Built Villas. £765 Leasehold, £930 Freehold. Large Gardens. Facilities for Garage.

But on the Northwick Estate prices range from £1,025 to £2,500 for "convenient, thoroughly well built, semi-detached and detached; 3, 4 and 5 bedrooms ..." houses on a rather select-sounding development.

Northwick Park Station was opened in 1923 to serve the needs of a new residential suburb which has sprung up since the war midway between Preston Road and the eastern slopes of Harrow Hill .... The estate is now owned by Captain Spencer Churchill. The Northwick Estate, which includes a very attractive old farmhouse on Woodcock Hill, and a considerable tract of land next to Ducker, the Harrow School bathing place, is being laid out with exceptional care.

The houses are generously treated in respect of garden space, and in addition to the Northwick Park Golf Club, which forms part of the estate, a recreation ground of five acres, known as the Palaestra, has been provided for tennis with an attractive pavilion or club house. The course of the Harrow Golf Club adjoins the property on the south side, and adds to the amenities of the new suburb. *[ML 1928]*

116

Two golf clubs, tennis at the Palaestra and and the involvement of the aristocracy. Metro-land bliss! According to the *Oxford Classical Dictionary*, a Palaestra was "a low building with a central courtyard in the interior covered with fine sand, and rooms about it for undressing and washing ... especially used by boys who were there taught the rules of wrestling". I wonder if it is still there!

By 1932:

> There are now many Harrows – North, South, West Etc. – but there is one Harrow-on-the Hill.

and *Metro-land* wants to have its cake and eat it, waxing lyrical about what has been "secured against the tides of change", though with a note of realism at the end:

> This is the Harrow of the windy ridge and the village street, happily well secured now against the tides of change which have swept over "the exceeding rich and fruitful fields" which a writer of 1659 described as lying "for a long way together" under Harrow Hill. Even in 1831, a century ago, the entire population of Harrow with Wealdstone and Greenhill was only 3,861. That represents about the annual increase of the population of the same district today ....

> The view from the churchyard is famous, but its beauty has suffered much of late.

Northwick Park has been growing rapidly and in a model way.

> Northwick Park Station, opened as recently as 1923, has been completely rebuilt to serve the needs of a new residential suburb, which in the last five years has grown at the rate of nearly a thousand houses a year. The whole area between the

117

Metropolitan Railway and the Kenton cross roads has been developed on the most attractive modern lines and might well serve other local authorities as a model of town planning.

But North Harrow is felt to score for modernity and the amenities required of a new suburb. *Metro-land* is certainly feeling positive again about "the tides of change"!

North Harrow has grown up round the Metropolitan Station – now an up-to-date building of the latest type. The changes effected here in the last five years have been as remarkable as any in the outer London area, the population having more than doubled. The old high road from Harrow to Pinner is unrecognisable at this point save for the sharp rectangular turn at the now forgotten Hooking Bridge Green. It has become a broad and comely High Street. On both sides of the line attractive avenues are being laid out with pleasant vistas and gardening would seem to be a universal hobby. On the south side a fine new 80ft. wide arterial road will ultimately be carried through to Ealing. North Harrow may congratulate itself on being born late, when it compares its amenities with those of any London suburb which was developed even a dozen years ago.

Not far away, Rayners Lane [more marketable without the apostrophe?] "awaits development" no more. Development is so fast, and so well planned, that it is worth frequent trips just to see it grow, even if you are not interested in buying!

Nowhere in the whole perimeter of London has more remarkable development taken place during the past year than at Rayners Lane, the station for Harrow Garden Village. It repays a visit at short intervals to see it grow.

The new township is rising fast, and there will be no occasion here to lament in future a failure of foresight in town-planning. The progress is most rapid on the north side of the railway.

The axis is not the line of old Rayners Lane, but rather the splendid new arterial road which is being laid out straight from the station to North Harrow Station on the main Metropolitan line. It will be linked with Northolt and Ealing on the one side and with Wealdstone on the other.

The aggregate frontage disposed of already exceeds 25,000 feet and sales of houses at all prices are being effected in increasing volume.

The essential amenities are listed:

Shops and schools have already made their appearance. Churches and a cinema are to follow.

It may be called a Garden Village but in reality it has the advantage of being part of a continuous built-up area!

West Harrow, North Harrow and Harrow Garden Village are already in touch, and the new Pinner Village is beckoning at short range to Harrow Garden Village at the other end of Rayners Lane.

If the quiet rustic beauty of old Rayners Lane is now a memory of the past, like the picturesque farm-house, the broad streets of the new suburb are being beautified by the planting of trees.

So that's all right then. A few trees are enough to compensate for what has been lost. But despite this enthusiasm for development and casual acceptance of the demolition of the "picturesque farm-house", the writer still feels able to talk happily about Headstone Manor being "saved" from being "swallowed up"!

Headstone Farm is now almost swallowed up by the houses which have risen around it. ... The place was saved by the public spirit of the Hendon Rural District Council which has bought some 60 acres of land adjoining and laid them out as a recreation ground.

The Garden Village is the Met's own baby and is listed under "The Estates":

Harrow Garden Village, Rayners Lane. An estate of some 213 acres extending from south of Rayners Lane station towards Pinner, with over 16 acres reserved for open spaces, tennis courts etc. The whole of the Roads have now been constructed ... .

A glance at the map suggests that these open spaces are rather round the fringes and that the development looks fairly solid, but I will be finding out what it feels like on the ground.

Under "Other Housing Developments" are other mentions of activity at Rayners Lane. It appears that the estate is unspoiled because building has not started!

Rayners Lane [for Harrow Garden Village]. A delightful unspoiled residential estate with great future prospects; over 1600 houses programmed for.

Coming to the advertisements, Northwick Park still sounds nice, though one wonders what shape the "old hamlet of Preston" was in by then. It is interesting to note that the farmhouse has had to go.

Woodcock Dell Estate, Northwick Park
The Estate is actually the site of the old Woodcock Dell Farmhouse and nearby is Kenton and the old hamlet of Preston.
[H Gibson, Metropolitan Railway Surplus Lands Committee]

120

But look what you get on the Harrow Garden Estate, according to "A Personal Statement by E.S. Reid"!

... E.S. Reid's estate has the particular advantage of being *self-contained* and wherever you choose a house on this estate you may rest assured that you will be surrounded by other of E.S. Reid's houses, and by that it is intended to convey that you may be sure that you will not have a cheap mass production house anywhere near you to lower the value of your own property.

In developing this section [immediately adjoining Rayners Lane Station entrance] *great care has been exercised*, without regard of expense, to keep right away from the monotony of mass production houses which are so swiftly covering the suburbs of London. *It must appeal* to every-one in choosing their house that their selection on this Estate provides them with something different from 99 per cent of their friends and relatives. Furthermore, this particular *variety of types* must certainly create a much more lasting value.

In developing E.S. Reid's Estate *profit has not been the first consideration*. The first object has been to produce an area that will not be a blot on the landscape and a district where purchasers may *feel proud* of their own Estate ...

On this Estate proof is offered of cases where houses are moved to protect trees and hedges *not* as is usually the case trees and hedges moved to make way for a few extra houses ...

At the moment there are no less than 16 different types to choose from ...

There are no useless or unnecessary gadgets ...

[£895–£1,350 Freehold]

This really is something and I look forward to seeing it. It seems to promise more than the Robinson equivalent:

121

A. Robinson, Harrow Garden Village

A House in a Hundred

Yes, a house in a hundred, and its *[sic]* true! Planned to please; built to last and sold at prices that are definitely "rock bottom". [£875 to £1,150 Freehold] [ML 1932]

Back in time to 1924, and Harper paints a charming picture of "old" Harrow.

... Harrow is a little hilltop microcosm; complete in itself. From the pleasant pastures, that still ring the hilltop round, the cows and sheep crop the succulent grass, and break in upon the more hushed portions of service in the parish church with a mingled chorus of "Moo-oo" and "Baa-a"; while parliaments of rooks and crows in windy tree-tops vie with the chatter and shouting of the playgrounds.

But Harper is also surprisingly [particularly in a book about "Rural Nooks"] positive about the new.

All around Harrow, but especially towards the south and west, modern facilities in journeying to and from London have opened up districts that have until now been devoted entirely to agriculture. Greenhill, that was a mere hamlet, is becoming populous: the new railway stations of Sudbury Town, Sudbury Hill and South Harrow are the centres whence modern villas, each with its own garden, spread; and Roxeth ... has ceased to be a weakly offshoot and has come, thanks to the South Harrow station, to be a place whence it is not difficult to travel in the morning, nor impossible to return late at night. A new era has dawned for Roxeth, as well as for Wood End to the south-west of it. *[RNR]*

Maxwell in 1927 talks about a Headstone Manor that is still a wonder, but one under threat.

It is not unnatural to suppose that the existence of a wonderful moated grange, centuries old and standing in a romantic spot of many acres, through which a pathway runs where anyone may pass, would be known to dwellers within less than a mile of it; and yet when I enquired for the Moat Farm at Headstone in the suburban roads that lie north-west of Harrow-on-the-Hill station six persons had no idea of the whereabouts of the place and the seventh sent me in the wrong direction. Yet all of these persons could probably have told me without hesitation where the nearest public house or picture palace lay! ...

It is one of the most picturesque places in the Home Counties ...

There are several houses round London where the remains of a moat, long since dry, can be traced, but this old farm at Headstone is the only one I know, with the single exception of that at Eltham, where the actual water of the moat still encircles the building, and as a farm, carried on as such, it is, I think, unique.

Behind *[the]* barn is the orchard, and surrounding the whole farm are some sixty acres of meadows and woodland.

Moat Farm is rapidly becoming an oasis; new houses and roads are fast encroaching on the land around, but the merciful protection of the fine old trees that circle the place shut off nearly all signs of this "improvement" of the countryside. Once within this truly magic circle, but ten miles from London, all sense of modern life is easily crowded out of the mind by the memories and still existing realities of an old English yesterday.

He sees some hope for the farm but ends with a plea:

The fate of Moat Farm seems at present to be in the lap of the gods. Just now it is carrying on as a farm, just as it has for so many centuries, but change is in the air and something will have to happen soon. The flood of bricks and mortar will engulf its fields till they finally sweep away the house too, unless an effort is made to rescue the old place from the march of "progress". There is some talk, I believe, of trying to preserve the estate by turning the fields into a public park and the house into a museum and library.

If this should come to be, I hope that whoever has charge of it ... will not destroy the private estate look with asphalt paths, iron railings and ugly bandstands .... *[JBL]*

In 1932 *London and Suburbs* is taking its usual positive view of development, starting with Harrow Garden Village:

Nowhere in the whole perimeter of London has more remarkable development taken place, during the past year, than at Harrow Garden Village, and already there is definite evidence that this desirable district will develop into one of the most popular residential areas around London.

The planning of the estate, which comprises some 213 acres of well-timbered land, is on particularly generous lines, with wide avenues, circles, closes and open spaces, tennis courts, recreation grounds and reservations for churches and chapels. Every care is being bestowed on its development to permanently assure its natural beauty and to render it delightful for all time from all aspects ....

From a health point of view the district leaves nothing to be desired. On all sides are green fields and rural lanes; the air clean and refreshing ....

This is not the image of Rayners Lane in my mind's eye, but I intend to look at it afresh. Likewise with the "delightful" North Harrow:

124

This is a delightful modern and healthy district ... surrounded on all sides by beautiful country, and where one can breathe pure, clean and refreshing air.

The shopping facilities are really excellent, with modern up-to-date shops, and every form of outdoor and indoor sports, recreation and amusements are well catered for, leaving nothing to be desired.

Whilst an advertisement offers:

Freehold Houses of Distinction on the Bessborough Estate, Blenheim Road, North Harrow, £695

... English Roofing Tiles and Bricks used Throughout. *[LAS]*

A strong copy claim indeed, but it is time for the Briggs antidote to builders' hyperbole:

... "The Hill" ... is still very largely monopolised by the school, but it is becoming more and more an island surrounded by an endless sea of "Distinctive Homes". ... in order to keep itself unspotted from the world and, by preserving its rural amenities, to maintain a steady flow of fee-payers, the school has had to buy large tracts of land on the skirts of the hill where it stands. These purchases have been of great value to the rapidly growing district of Harrow ..., for they have secured open spaces which, if not actually public, do greatly enhance the attractions of the neighbourhood. The nightingale still returns every spring to the wooded slopes of Harrow Hill.

Briggs certainly takes the view that the school was the saviour of some of Harrow's greenery and is rightly unconcerned about the motives. One way and another, money is a recurring theme. He then launches into critique and attack on the whole concept of Metro-land.

Nearly all the area in the new *[Harrow]* district, except the wooded belt in the north, was given up to pasture up to a few years ago; but now the cattle are everywhere being displaced by estate agents' screaming placards and builders' growling concrete mixers. The Metropolitan Railway is a modern upstart [compared with the L.N.W.R. and L.M.S.R.] but has had a far greater influence on the development of the town because from its outset it has made full use of such slogans as "Metroland", "Beechy Bucks" and the like, to tempt people to live in the country that its servants have done so much to obliterate. The pages of "Metroland", one of its publications, are filled with irresistible pictures of country lanes, rustic stiles, and thatched cottages bowered in roses – just the very things that the motorist and the house agent and the builder have practically destroyed throughout the nearer parts of "Metroland" itself. It may be highly beneficial to humanity, as it certainly is to the pockets of shareholders, that these vast migrations should take place; but the language of hyperbole so freely employed in the process jars upon a sensitive ear, and even the helpless victims of the campaign must feel some regret in seeing the countryside receding so rapidly from them. The recent extension of the "Met" to Canons Park and Stanmore will certainly expedite the movement.

On my continuing travels I will as ever be trying to look with the eyes of the "helpless victims". They were in any case being helped by external forces countering the enthusiasm and excesses of the developers:

> ... at the 1931 census *[the population]* leaped up to 96,984, ... showing an increase of about 100% in ten years. So far as one can judge, this rate of progress is continuing at the present time, and it may be some satisfaction to the builders of "Houses of Charm and Character" [as they are known in this refined neighbourhood] to realize that the area of the district

126

can accommodate 600,000 people on the luxurious basis of twelve houses to the acre.

At least that would be the position if no allowance were made for open spaces. But fortunately the local fathers have long been aware of needs in that direction and have prepared town-planning schemes by which provision has been made for ample reservations .... Add to these public spaces – over 1000 acres in all – the enormous area of the proposed "Green Girdle" and the 400 acres or so acquired by the governors of Harrow School, and it is clear that a substantial portion of this beautiful district is safe for all time. *[MON]*

Holmes has little to add this time.

The growth of the little town on "The Hill" to the west thereof has reversed the usual order of urban expansion and this side is distinctly not its best. Only in the neighbourhood immediately to the east, and on the actual slopes leading up to Harrow church and school do the ancient amenities linger. And although the graceful outline of the twin hills – that to the south being Sudbury – is very pleasing from the meadows around Uxbridge, the only good near view of the spire-crowned height is from the east .... The new buildings and the school chapel line the brow of the hill upon this side, and the church appears to rise from among them. Below are noble banks of trees and a green declivity, though the foreground of hedgerow and flat meadowlands, vast stretches of white and gold in the spring and early summer, will soon give way to the ubiquitous builder.

The epitaph in *The King's England* is rather downbeat.

The view the poet loved has changed in this great Age of Change. Not even Harrow with its Prime Ministers can stop the spoiler. The towers of Windsor still rise in the distance, but a great gasholder has thrust itself into the view and a sea of red-roofed houses comes surging up to the green belt round the hill.

... the old town has spread itself until today it covers 12,000 acres with a population marching on towards two hundred thousand; into its municipal area have been drawn a dozen old villages and hamlets ...

From the churchyard, spreading out beyond the playing-fields, is a vista of rows and rows of houses of Greater London, for Harrow has drawn to itself in our time such places as South Harrow, North Harrow, Harrow Weald, Greenhill, Roxeth, Pinner and Pinner Green, Hatch End and Rayner's Lane, Kenton, Wealdstone, Headstone and the two Stanmores. All these fragments of old Middlesex and bits of new London make up the twenty square miles of Greater Harrow. *[KEM]*

But what does Harrow [or more correctly the Harrows] look like today? To find out, I make my first Harrow expedition, to Headstone Manor, on a nice, sunny Sunday afternoon in mid September. The way the sun is burning down it feels more like July or early August. Over the field next to the car park I can see the looming buildings and chimneys of the Kodak factory. In the other direction I look across the moat to where I would be able to see the Manor House, if it wasn't for the plastic sheeting that covers it while restoration is carried out. The moat itself looks fairly murky, with a lot of people deciding that it makes a good place to dump their rubbish, but the ducks seem to be swimming happily enough and I can see a huge goldfish [carp I suppose!] so perhaps it is not as dirty as it looks. I can just see the bridge that crosses the moat from what was the farmyard to the house. To the left as I walk towards the yard I can see a cricket match in process, a traditional enough "rural" English scene. The farmyard and house now form the Harrow Museum and Heritage Centre and several of the buildings have been brought here in recent times, but the great barn is the original and forms the focal point of the museum. I can hear music coming from it, as usual on a Sunday lunchtime. It appears that, due to the current stage of restoration, it is no longer possible to cross the bridge to the house, which is a shame as you used to be able to see a 1930s-style living room, a touch of nostalgia, and pictures of houses and the ads for them, which were highly relevant to the theme of this book.

Beyond the farmyard area there is what is now unmistakeably, and against Maxwell's wishes, a public park, with rather run down looking swings and a graffiti-covered changing room, a fairly typical example of a council's lack of concern, money or both. I will take a look round to see if I can get a feel for what it once was, but I am not very hopeful. Behind the barn and beyond the tennis courts are some real Metroland semis, looking quite pretty amongst the trees. There is nobody playing on the tennis courts, perhaps surprisingly on such a nice day. Now back to the very typical park and Headstone Lane, where some friends of my parents used to live, the oldest of whose children was a rather nice blonde girl called Pam, to whom I became rather attracted as we grew older. We held hands once but nothing came of it, though I used to dream of this place. I could get quite poetic – shame I'm no Betjeman! More cricket pitches over here, one with a game in progress, one with the wickets pitched ready for the start. If I look towards Harrow-on-the Hill I can see fields and trees and get some small feeling of what it was like here as countryside, though the overall ambience remains suburban. One really does get an impression of the greenery of the Hill standing firm against a tide of red roofs swirling around its foothills.

As I walk back, the dominant feature is the Kodak factory. A good source of employment ever since it opened in 1890, but not conducive to a rural [or even Metro-land] reverie. Back at the moat I see an enormous brown rat. Lovely! Things do not pick up much either, because as I drive away, I am immediately plunged into that tide of suburbia. From here to Eastcote and beyond, it is semis all the way, with very few breaks.

I do not visit Harrow proper until a bright cold morning in late November. I reach the Hill on the return trip via Ruislip, Eastcote and Rayners Lane, at least along the main road the epitome of suburbia as monotony, but once I arrive the air is fresh and the houses are distinctive, in a variety of styles but mostly saying "money". There are some wonderful houses up here and I notice that I have parked opposite one called Herga House, a version of the Anglo Saxon name for Harrow, a tall, narrow, very Victorian building in which one could imagine Lewis Carroll living and Alice commencing her adventures. Through the yard entrance to my left I can look over the roofs of the town to the valley. You can certainly see a long way from here, even today when, despite the brightness, there is a certain amount of haze. I start by going down Harrow Park, which Foley called "a retired spot where we may enjoy visions of woody slopes, or a bright expanse of green meadows stretching away towards Hampstead and Highgate". I am glad that I did not bring the car as a notice on the wall says "Harrow Park. Private Road. No Unauthorised Parking. Warning: vehicles without parking permits will have wheel clamps attached. Charge for removal £25". Cheaper than parking in Pinner, though, as will be seen in due course.

Perhaps surprisingly, a great deal of the view is still here. The absence of leaves on the trees means that I can see the Northwick Park Hospital to the left, but if this was the summer the prospect would look even more unspoiled. It would be lovely to live here. There is a pretty little footpath winding down the hill, strewn with leaves and with two notices at its start. One says "You are entering a nature

130

conservation area. Please keep to the footpaths. Keep dogs on leads. Respect all wild animals and plants". But underneath it says "Private. Harrow School Golf Club Members Only", so I am not sure if the first notice is addressed solely to that [presumably] select group. There is a wonderfully ornate chalet-style house amongst the trees which looks intriguing, but there are other places to see and I resist the temptation to explore further. A big red building has a sign on it saying "Newlands" [I assume one of the school houses] and a rugby ball on the lawn in front of it, which is quite appropriate as this is the week after England have won the World Cup! [Like Sussex winning the County Championship, this was an event I wondered if I would ever see. 2003 is an *annus mirabilis* indeed. What next? The Ashes?!] The hospital has spoiled the view somewhat, but it is still lovely.

Back on the High Street on the left is "The King's Head Hotel, established 1535", but it is boarded up and, I believe, being converted to housing, presumably of the "luxury apartment" type. A poor exchange for one of Middlesex's historic inns. I walk past Bradby's, I suppose another house of the school, Union flag in the window and a picture of Jonny Wilkinson. Some of the boys come towards me along the street and I see that they wear their boaters even in the winter. Except for the traffic, itself not too intrusive at this time of day, I imagine that this street has really changed very little since the time of even the earliest observers that I have quoted. Not much change from more recent times either, with the Old Etonian restaurant still here, where a waiter accidentally sprayed champagne over my wife on her birthday soon after we met, twenty years ago.

Looking down West Street I reflect that this view really did change during the course of the last century, because through the mist I can see so-called North Harrow, and there seems to be a great deal of it. The street itself, though, cannot have changed much, consisting as it does largely of Victorian

131

cottages, with some larger houses further down. It is a quarter past eleven and the boys are streaming along for a change in lesson, all in their dark blue blazers and straw hats. Is this really their winter garb? Perhaps the school decrees that winter does not start until January!

I have now reached the main part of the school, the core of which is Tudor but with many Victorian buildings. It is not within the scope of this account to give a detailed description of them over and above those quoted earlier. I do not believe that much will have changed, on the outside anyway, as except for the parked cars there is a timeless quality about it. There is even a master in his gown, shades of my own distant school days but standing out in the 21st century. No mortar board, though, so not a real Mr Chips. The notice on the side of the Tudor building says "The Old Schools. This is the original building at Harrow, finished in 1615" [so not strictly speaking Tudor after all then!] "and enlarged in 1820".

Now into the churchyard, wondering why I have never done this before, and to the "Byron" [Peachey] grave. A notice says "This was the favourite spot of Lord Byron whilst a pupil at Harrow School between 1801 and 1805. It was here, surrounded by reminders of mortality, that he invoked a more melancholy and reflective Muse. To this place he often came to escape the restraints of school life. He would sit for hours and hours gazing at the view from the top of the Peachey stone". Looking at the grave with its protective bars, and the church and the churchyard beyond, it all seems very quiet and beautiful and, I suppose, much as Byron would have seen it. Looking out, there is a direction finder, stating that "This indicator was provided through the generosity of the Friends of Harrow Church and erected by the Harrow Urban District Council that many might the more enjoy this view". The indicator shows what I might be looking at, though it is far too misty today to have any chance of seeing such faraway places as Wendover, Guildford or Oxford. In fact, beyond the greenery of the Hill I am more conscious of the suburban landscape and the tube train beetling across it. There is a public footpath to Bessborough Road and it would be nice to walk down there, though on the other side of it is what was named West Harrow, merging seamlessly with North Harrow and then into Rayners Lane, so even if I could see to the distant green fields today I would be taking in a lot of Metro-land in between.

I am really glad that I did this. The birds are singing and the rooks are cawing, albeit in competition with the constant hum of the traffic down below. I can see this as some of our authors see it, as an island with its lovely old trees, the church and the school standing firm against the previously strong tide of suburbanisation [or villafication]. Indeed, over to the east the view is even more built up than in the west, with tower blocks in the mist in the distance.

Walking down the hill to the town to have some lunch, I see a notice on the wall saying "Take heed. The first recorded motor accident in Great Britain involving the death of the driver occurred on Grove Hill on 25th February 1899. This plaque was unveiled on the seventieth anniversary by the Mayor of Harrow Alderman Charles Stenhouse". I think that I was vaguely aware of this but it seems to need a special reason to explore places so close to home. On my right is Football Lane. It would be all right walking down it before a match but harder work coming back up afterwards. As I walk there are more wonderful large Victorian buildings, mostly I imagine owned by the school, and I get a view over a rather overgrown meadow to the football and rugby pitches, but in reality as I get lower everything tends to be dominated by the useful but utilitarian buildings of Northwick Park Hospital. So modernity soon creeps up and the view of the town is marred by some naff modern blocks, but reassuringly I can see beyond them the wooded part of Harrow Weald around Old Redding.

Approaching the town, Kenton Road contains some rather nondescript buildings, but there is a quaint fingerpost sign saying "Wembley 3, London 10". Looked at from here, to call central [non-Hill] Harrow an architectural jumble would be to flatter it. As I cross the railway tracks that helped to open it up in the first place I wonder what went wrong here, as in so many other British towns and cities, to produce quite such a dog's breakfast. The St Ann's shopping centre has some good stores, and a very useful Gents, but it is totally anonymous and could be anywhere.

I have now scuppered myself for more exploring by buying some books required for Christmas presents, and after a quick beer and sandwich I set off back. I walk along Grove Hill Road just for a little change of scene. It does not seem to go very far but gives a different view of the Hill, though with the winter sun low behind it, it is not easy to see. As I walk up there is a spinney on one side and some interesting Edwardian houses on the other, probably again belonging to the school. The impression up here, again, is that everything carries on much as it ever did and that nothing much has changed in the last 150 years. I go up a twitten towards the church; "Public Footpath no. 71", reminding me how organised things are in Harrow. There is a little garden behind the wall and you really would not know that you were in the heart of suburbia. To maintain the mood, I walk back across the churchyard, and looking towards the west it occurs to me that somewhere over there in the haze is Ickenham, as I can certainly see to here from the back of my house. I read the words on the stone in front of "Byron's" tomb and record a few of them to try to preserve a feeling for the timeless quality of this magical place: "Oh! as I trace again thy winding hill, Mine eyes admire, my heart adores thee still, Thou drooping elm! Beneath whose boughs I lay, And frequent mus'd the twilight hours away". Didn't he have to go back to school? As I have already said, looking out in any direction you see development, but within time has stood still. I stop on the terrace just outside the Old Schools, next to a sign down saying "The Hundred Steps. Please exercise extreme caution when negotiating these steps". Visibility is now a little better and I can see more semis. How lovely it must have been before they were there! After the scruffy anonymity of the town centre, and being back amongst these venerable buildings and the boys in their rugby gear, I again feel in a time warp. It has certainly spoiled me for any more exploration today as I cannot face the contrast with Greenhill or the Metro-land developments, which will have to await another fine day.

Of course, I cannot get off this magical island without traversing a piece of suburbia, so I decide to bite on the bullet and head for Roxeth. Driving towards it I can see the little terraces of Greenhill, so decried in one of the books, and then stop at the bottom of West Street, gaining an interesting view of the village on the Hill. I find that I have stopped by a horse trough, a nice memory of times gone by. Then I pass the gasworks and I am really back on the plain, in a rather dreary townscape in an even drearier shopping street, albeit with a very diverse community.

The next morning finds me in Cornwall Road, near North Harrow station and on the Headstone Estate. The houses are pre-WW1 terraced, all right in their way but perhaps not doing justice to what must have been beautiful surroundings at the time they were built. Delayed by a dustcart, I take a walk down the road, noting the Kodak chimney behind. The houses have been subject to a variety of treatments; whether they were all pebbledashed to begin with I don't know but some are now, whilst others have their brickwork painted rather garishly. At this time of year, with the sun low in the sky, the overall impression is rather dark and gloomy, with continuous stretches of houses with very small front gardens and the parked cars on either side of the road contributing to a somewhat cramped feel.

135

Back in the car, I come out by the parish church of St George, Headstone, which is on higher ground, giving a more open feel, and down the road there is a lovely view to the fields and trees of Harrow Weald Common. Again, most of the housing here is pre-WW1, another reminder of how much development there was in Middlesex before the Metro-land period. I turn into Bolton Road, which is fairly wide and tree-lined, but again there are cars parked on either side because the houses have no garages and the gardens are not big enough for parking, meaning that as soon as I turn away from the views of the countryside it all feels rather enclosed. Before leaving Headstone I feel I ought to take a closer look at the Kodak factory that so dominates the area. The pub where I turn is called the Goodwill to All, a pleasant name and one that I hope reflects the feelings of its patrons when leaving on a Friday night. It is not until I start driving along-side the factory that I realise quite how big it is, certainly not pretty but an important part of the area. Once I cross the railway line, no doubt one of the reasons for siting the factory here in the first place, I am confronted by council and other housing of the rather undistinguished nature one expects to find near factories. Definitely not the most scenic part of Harrow, but again with the saving grace of the views to Grim's Dyke and Harrow Weald Common. Driving back, the vast bulk of the factory and its surroundings on the left provide an industrial landscape that is not quite Lowry but certainly not rural Middlesex, though on the right is an entrance to the Headstone Manor grounds.

Back in North Harrow I park at the bowling alley, because I want to take a walk round and see what impression I get. The shopping area is depressing, partly because some of the shops are boarded up and the road side of the bowling alley is only marginally less tatty than the car park side, but also because of the by now familiar jumble of architectural styles. All in all it does not match very well the fine words written

136

about it in *London and Suburbs*. I notice that Wealdstone Motors boasts a rather distinctive inter-war style but the overall effect is not pleasing. Behind the bowling alley it is rather dark and gloomy but I want to take a look at Hooking Green, which proves to live up to its name with a nice green with trees in the middle and houses round it, some small semis and some terraced, the overall effect being somewhat marred by the widely differing levels and styles of maintenance from which they have benefited. I try to allow for the fact that even on a sunny day things can look darker and more oppressive at this time of year but none the less it is hard to think of these surroundings as inspiring. Can one really agree with the *Metro-land* copywriter that "North Harrow may congratulate itself on being born late, when it compares its amenities with those of any London suburb ...'"?

I head towards Harrow Garden Village down Suffolk Road, which has some good detached houses as well as semis and open space behind, through which according to the map flows Yeading Brook, though I cannot actually see it. The Garden Village itself has an interesting variety of houses, including some that are Arts and Crafts influenced and some "moderne" and has a pleasant feel to it, with trees, albeit of suburban sort, along the roads. I see through a gate that there are some allotments to provide a rather traditional touch and beyond them more houses, nice enough but too many of them. None the less the effect is much better than the one that you get on the main road. It more or less comes up to scratch as a garden village, though one without shops unless you head for Rayners Lane station in the south-eastern corner. Down Dewsbury Close there are some pleasant houses round a little green space with trees in the middle, though again there is the consciousness of other houses pressing in behind. Downs Avenue is rather improbably named, but the bungalows along it perhaps provide a very indirect connection with my beloved Sussex. The Streamside Open Space is disappointing, hemmed

137

in by the backs of houses, never the best side to look at, and graffiti-covered garages, and littered with rubbish, a rather forlorn reminder of what was here not so long ago The brook itself is full of cardboard boxes, Safeway magazines [soon to be a rarity], beer cans and other gubbins. Why don't the Garden Villagers appreciate what they have, or could have? However, my spirits do lift as I walk back, with some of the houses indeed looking very pleasant in the sunshine and the atmosphere quieter than one might anticipate.

Before leaving Harrow I decide to go upmarket a little to the Northwick Estate. Woodcock Dell Avenue has some nice bungalows ending in open space, albeit next to the Met line, and a view of the trees on Barn Hill in Wembley. Up Woodcock Hill there are some fairly substantial detached houses and some posh-sounding road names like Mount Stewart Avenue. Stopping the car at the brow of the hill I look down The Ridgeway to the west but only gain a partial view of Harrow-on-the-Hill due, once more, to the looming bulk of Northwick Park Hospital in the way. It does still have a pleasant feel to it, even though the road itself is rather busy. There are some prosperous-looking detached Tudorbethan houses and ahead views to Stanmore and beyond. I move on to Woodcock Park. Presumably this is where the "Palaestra" was, but it does not look enormously exciting at first sight. Then it seems to have something of a *Blow Up* feeling to it, or perhaps this is just in my mind because David Hemmings died recently. There are houses backing on to it and the tennis courts seem to be in reasonable nick. Woodcock Park Lodge is quite interesting and adjoins the Kenton Synagogue. The Wealdstone Brook here is not inspiring, running between brick walls and with an up-ended buggy in the water; hopefully no baby in it when it went in, and sundry other rubbish. Depressing, and another wasted opportunity. Uxendon Manor Primary School reminds me that I am not far from some of the ground covered on the Wembley tour.

138

I return home via Rayners Lane, the "centre" of which contains some distinctively 1930s buildings, including a "Holden" station, but the overall effect is rather scruffy, with the usual jumble of styles. Not the ideal note on which to leave Harrow, but overall it still has plenty going for it.

Further reading

Harrow Through The Ages Walter W. Druett, The Hillingdon Press, 1934

The Stanmores and Harrow Weald Through The Ages Walter W. Druett, The Hillingdon Press, 1938

The Book of Harrow E.D.W. Chaplin, Staples Press, 1948

The Story of Roxeth T.L. Bartlett, Fox Publications, 1948

Harrow before your time Pinner and Hatch End W.E.A. Local History Group, 1972

Harrow walkabout Elizabeth Cooper, Pinner and Hatch End W.E.A., 1973

The Countryside Lies Sleeping Alan W. Ball, The Riverhill Press, 1981

Harrow, A Pictorial History Dennis F. Edwards, Phillimore, 1993

Pinner, Hatch End, North Harrow and Rayners Lane, A Pictorial History Patricia A. Clarke, Phillimore, 1994

A Lookback At Harrow Don Walter, Orpheus, 1995

The Archive Photographs Series, Harrow Brian Girling, Chalford, 1996

Harrow Past Eileen M. Bowlt, Historical Publications, 2000

6

Leafy Pinner

Finally we come to the village whose image has perhaps changed the least. It was "nice" in the time that Betjeman was describing and it still sounds "nice" now. "Leafy" and "Pinner" seem to go together. Again I will be assessing the image against the current reality.

As Thorne makes clear back in 1876, Pinner started with the advantage of a centre that was bettered, if at all, only by Harrow.

Pinner stands on elevated ground, whence flows one of the feeders of the Colne. The main street is broad, clean, lined, among many modern ones, with several old half-timber houses, with overhanging upper floors and gables. On its N. side is a long, low, old country inn, an excellent specimen of its class, the Queen's Head, bearing on its front the date 1705, and no doubt a genuine relic of Queen Anne's reign. At the upper [E.] end of the street, on the highest ground, soars the weather-beaten church tower, with the bare trunk of a huge elm before it, fitting finish to a scene unusually archaic, rustic, and pictur-esque for its nearness to London.

Pinner Green is a sort of hamlet, half a mile N. of the vill. Beyond are Pinner Grove and Woodhall.

As in Harrow, the advent of the London and North Western Railway had already caused some development, though I wonder how many residents of present-day Hatch End are aware of its early claim to fame as a landing place for coal:

> Woodridings, one and a half miles, by the Railway Station, is a growing hamlet, with some good residences and a chapel-of-ease. ... Hatch End by the rly. 1 mile north of the vill., is a hamlet of small houses, with a landing-place for coals on the rly. *[HEL]*

Thorne mentions the various distinguished houses such as Pinner Wood Park but has relatively little to say about the countryside, an omission remedied by Foley fourteen years later. By this time the Met has arrived, opening up Pinner village itself for [initially at any rate] ramblers.

> From Roxeth a charming little green lane leads to Pinner village, in springtime passing between fragrant hedges of haw-thorn the greater part of the way.

> The new Metropolitan extension has opened up a most interesting district for the pedestrian. It runs past Pinner and the journey thither from Baker Street can be accomplished any half-hour. The station is planted in the heart of the brisk little village; and a few yards off is the broad main street, which slopes to a brooklet hidden by a queer old bridge of a single arch.

Pinner Park was, and is, one of Pinner's glories.

> ... a footpath through Pinner Park gives us a fine open walk, commanding ample views of the surrounding country. From the farm at the further end, a continuing path beside a lane takes us to the London and North-Western Railway; and, crossing this by a footbridge, we are at the hamlet of Hatch End. Right opposite us, under the trees, is the commencement of another footpath; and by its means we are led through a

succession of fertile meadows, arriving in about a mile at Harrow Weald.

It is of course no longer possible to get to Harrow "almost entirely by fields", nor even to Pinner Green, though according to my *Country Walks No.1* book published by the Met the latter was possible at least until 1929.

We need never be at a loss for a stroll in the neighbourhood of Pinner. Beside these meadowpaths, the rambler may make his way from Pinner to Harrow almost entirely by fields, and enjoy the different views of the church-crowned slope as he approaches it. Or he may strike out northwards and explore the Pinner and Oxhey woods on the high ground a couple of miles to the north-west of the village.

The walking possibilities were endless, notwithstanding Hatch End's "neat little erections":

From the *[Headstone]* Manor Farmyard beside some picturesque old farm buildings, we pass onto a road with green borders on either hand, evidently another of the approaches to the manor in the days of its archiepiscopal splendour, and from this we drop into an exquisite little lane. We double and twist about with this till it crosses the railway and we come upon the little outlying hamlet of Hatch End, a collection of neat little modern erections interspersed with several old cottages, probably less comfortable, but certainly more picturesque. An old-fashioned, three-gabled, farmhouse, set behind trim lawns and ablaze with scarlet creeper, strikes us on the left, and passing through a row of stalwart elms we reach almost directly a road crossing our own. *[OLM]*

Walford paints a picture of a place with some development but not much.

143

It is a busy and thriving village, the main street being broad, well paved and lighted with gas, and containing several respectable shops and private houses of modern growth, interspersed with many of a more picturesque antiquated appearance, of the lath-and-plaster style of building, with projecting storeys and gabled roofs. Not the least interesting among these houses is the "Queen's Head", an old-fashioned roadside tavern on the north side of the street .... .

The number of inhabitants is still increasing though not very rapidly.

Here we again encounter the "River" Pinn, or Pin, which we have come across a number of times in our travels.

The village is pleasantly located on the rising ground which forms the north-western side of the vale of Harrow, and from this elevated spot flows one of the feeders of the river Colne, a little rivulet, called the Pin, which is crossed at the bottom of the main street by an antiquated bridge of one arch.

There is no shortage of gentry.

In the neighbourhood of Pinner are several good seats and family residences. Pinner Hill ... lies away on the high ground to the north-west. ... The house stands in ornamental park grounds, and commands extensive views.

Pinner Grove, northward of the village, is approached through a fine avenue of elms, and stands in ornamental park-like grounds.

Pinner Park appears to have been formerly a district of some importance. ... The estate, however, has long been broken up and converted to agricultural purposes.

I wonder what Thorne meant by saying that Pinner Park

144

appeared to have been a "district of some importance"? To complete the picture:

> About half a mile north of the village is Pinner Green, and near at hand is an estate known as Wood Hall. Woodridings is a hamlet further to the north-east; it boasts of some good villa residences and a chapel-of-ease. *[GL]*

Firth in 1906 gives more of an impression of development, though it is difficult to judge whether this reflected the passage of a few years or merely his own perspective.

> ... the place dwindled in importance until quite recent years, when improved railway communications have led to the building of many villas of a good type. The village is thus rapidly extending into the fields. The country is charming on every side.

There is history here as well as class.

> At the foot of Pinner main street stands an old red brick school, and near by, across the bridge, at the fork of the road, are three houses in wooded grounds, built for the widows of officers ...

> To the S. of the station is a good house, Pinner Grove ...

> Pinner Hall lies to the N. of the village, between the church and the Pinner and Hatch End station of the North-Western Railway. Near by is the estate of Wood Hall, with fine poplars. The hamlet of Woodridings is now merged in the modern Hatch End. Here, in 1881, died Mrs. Horatio Nelson Ward ... daughter of Nelson and Lady Hamilton.

Pinner Park remains as it was.

145

Pinner Park lies between Nower Hill, Pinner, and Hatch End, and is a broad sweep of farm land with a substantial farmhouse lying in the centre. It retains its ancient name from the days when it was forest land and the Abbots of Westminster were its keepers.

But there is development to the west and north of Pinner and Hatch End station.

Hatch End proper, the old hamlet of the name, lies half a mile to the east of the station, and contains one or two good houses and a number of forlorn cottages dating from the construction of the railway. There is also an ancient and most picturesque three-gabled farmhouse, said to be haunted. The name of Hatch End signifies a gateway to the forest or enclosure, covering what is now Pinner Park .... To the west of the station, in what was the old hamlet of Woodridings, a pleasant little township of neat villas is springing up. So, too, to the north of the station, running up to the Watford Road, a large estate, known as Royston Park, has developed in the last ten years. ... Five hundred yards to the N.W. of the station the railway cuts through the ancient Grimm's Dyke. *[MF]*

Hope Moncrieff is inclined on the whole to take a positive view of Pinner's ability to cope with development, which is now being spurred by the Met as well as the main line.

Pinner is a good old village that has taken a vigorous new growth on the stalk of the Metropolitan Railway, rooted in the business quarters of London. It still keeps an air of rustic charm among the sophistications of villadom, and is ringed about with parks and pretty hamlets – Pinner Green further on the road, Eastcote to the south, Woodridings and Hatch End to the north, connected by crooked lanes and green paths, which, indeed, begin to be too often cut up by builders. Its heart may

146

be marked at the station of the Metropolitan line, which here plays the part of landlord as well as carrier. From the railway and the Pin brook, turns up the main street, showing some old houses, real and artificial, as it mounts to the Church, an ancient one, altered and restored with picturesque effect in its shady nook.

Walkers need to take care not to get lost in the wilds round about.

... I despair of my reader not to lose himself in the labyrinth of shady roads, muddy, grassy lanes and bowery paths that lead southwards and westwards from Pinner, through a delightful country difficult to describe without a repetition of hackneyed epithets. The best I can do is to recommend him to No. 1 of a little series of penny guides published at the booking offices of the Metropolitan Railway, in which he has a selection of the ways traced for him. ... But the advice I should give myself, if at leisure on a fine day, would simply be to get lost in a leafy maze dotted with guide-posts to keep one from going far astray. *[MFH]*

I have already referred to this booklet, which cost twopence by 1929. Between then and now the walks described have been almost entirely built over, but back in 1908 even *Where to Live* was fairly low key on the subject of housing development.

Pinner is a pleasant, thriving little village ... . The village is located on rising ground that forms the north-western side of Harrow Vale, and consists for the most part of a broad well-kept main street sloping down to the Pin. The street wears that charming aspect which a blending of old-time shops and dwellings and well-designed modern houses generally confers. Its picturesqueness is enhanced by the fine old parish church, with its handsome tower, which stands at the eastern or upper end.

147

... .today it is a ... a favourite residential neighbourhood, with many pleasant well-built modern houses within its boundary. *[WTL]*

Jerrold, though, recognises its new status as an "outer residential suburb":

Pinner ..., with its two railway stations, is expanding into a new villadom, but around it is still much rural attractiveness in open fields and tree-shaded lanes, while its wide village street, rising gently to the flint and stone church, with its old-fashioned shops and irregular houses, its picturesque Queen Anne inn [1705], has about it an air of old-world comfort and prosperity. Long before its development as one of the outer residential suburbs, the district was noted for the comfortable houses in which, at various times, men of note lived. *[HBI]*

In 1921 *Metro-land* treats its readers to a history lesson, with an emphasis on the impact of transport on local economies.

In the good old days when the stage coaches careered over the highways, Pinner was a place of some importance. It was a market town, and the succession of stage coaches which passed through it invested Pinner with a mild prosperity which, however, could not withstand the advent of the railways. On their appearance the market declined and the stage coaches grew fewer, until at length both disappeared.

It is, though, a history lesson with purpose and a hero.

In course of time, however, the Metropolitan Railway made rich reparation, not only restoring in ample measure all that had been taken away, but introducing new conditions under the influence of which Pinner has grown to a degree which, to its more ancient inhabitants, would have appeared inconceivable.

148

The blessings that the Met have brought are such that

Pinner is now mostly composed of villa residences, with a rural background. These houses have been spreading outward steadily in the direction of Harrow and Eastcote, as well as Pinner Hill and Hatch End.

And it is nothing if not environmentally aware:

A few years ago there was some destruction made in the grand elms, which are such a beautiful feature of Pinner's environment, and it is to be hoped this vandalism will not be repeated.

"The Estates" section shows that Metro-land has truly arrived, with developments on the Met's land round its own station.

The Cecil Park Estate and the Grange Estate at Pinner, are the property of the Metropolitan Railway Surplus Lands Committee, and a scheme of development is progressing which is appealing to a great number of purchasers.

The Cecil Park Estate has a footway entrance direct from the estate on to the railway platform, and the Grange Estate, on the north side of the line, is practically touching the station.

Is there such a thing as having your transport link too close? In any case, development is not just for the new property-owning classes. There is local authority housing too, albeit closer to North Harrow.

Housing schemes [Hendon R.D.C.]. Houses in course of erection at Hooking Green Bridge and Pinner Hill Road.

But the appeal to the day trippers is still there, along with the establishments to cater to their needs.

149

Ye Cocoa Tree Tea Gardens. The ideal resort for Pleasure Parties. Pleasant Tea Gardens. Spacious Hall. Accommodation for 150.

Waxwell Tea Gardens. Bridge Street. Excellent accommodation for parties up to 60 ... Ideal situation. *[ML 1921]*

By 1928 the Met view of history has changed. Transport is out and agriculture is in, and the role of the Met itself rather downplayed.

Until the coming of the Metropolitan Railway, Pinner was just a sleepy little village, living a secluded life of its own, and devoted to agricultural pursuits. Wheat of particularly excellent quality used to be grown in the neighbourhood, and in Victorian days there was a large stud farm here [Tilbury's] which supplied London with many of its best carriage horses and the Shires with some of their best hunters. The railway brought the village into close touch with London, and Pinner began to grow with great rapidity.

It is still spreading fast in all directions, towards Harrow, towards Hatch End and towards Eastcote. In a retired lane by Nower Hill there are some interesting old houses.

But there is still concern about those trees. It isn't "leafy Pinner" for nothing.

The woodman's axe has been ruthlessly swung among the grand elms, which are still a beautiful feature of Pinner's environment; those who lay out building estates ought to spare every fine tree they can.

There are still houses for sale near the station, at prices in the mid range, and you can build your own if you prefer.

Grange and Cecil Park Estates. These desirable Estates are situated on the North and South sides, respectively, of the Metropolitan line. Several attractive houses are for sale with vacant possession. There are Detached Houses from £1,300–£1,600 Freehold and many excellent Plots are available for the erection of Detached or Semi-detached houses, at £5 per foot frontage.

In an accompanying advertisement the Grange Estate boasted "Exceptionally Artistic Detached Residences". I look forward to seeing them, as they sound very Metro-land. But it is not just the Met developing.

One of the choicest districts in Metro-Land … Numerous houses available. Wide range of residential Estates. Low priced semi-detached houses for sale at Pinner Green.

And also over to the west at Cuckoo Hill, Telling Bros. are promising:

The City Man's Ideal Residential Suburb

Superior Freehold Villas and Spacious Building Plots for Sale

Good schools

Tennis Courts are on the Estate

Tennis courts no less. Always a sign of class, but I wonder if they are still there. Back in the village Ye Cocoa Tree is still there but no longer offering Tea Gardens:

Licensed for music and dancing … Noted for home-made cakes and strawberry teas. *[ML 1928]*

In 1932 comes the news that part at least of rural Pinner has been saved.

151

Pinner Park ... Only one large farm house has stood upon it from time out of mind and now the whole estate of 251 acres has been secured as an open space by the Hendon Rural District Council at a cost of more than £80,000, which it shares with the Middlesex County Council.

But there is more housing, at quite a range of prices, in the direction of Eastcote.

Cannon Croft Estate

£825–£1450 Freehold

The General Housing Co. Ltd. *[ML 1932]*

Ye Cocoa Tree is no longer listed, perhaps confirming Pinner as a residential suburb rather than as a base for country rambles. Its residential advantages are of course the theme of *London and Suburbs Old and New*.

A picturesque, pleasant and rapidly growing village ...

In the days of old it was just simply a "rural" village – a hamlet of Harrow. It has grown apace during recent years, and whilst retaining many quaint and old time features, such as Tudor houses, ancient and picturesque cottages, and a hostelry dating back to Queen Anne, today Pinner is a separate parish, modern, up-to-date, with a charming aspect, and is a favourite residential centre.

Thus, in the eye of the estate agent, Pinner manages to be both quaint and "modern and up-to-date". It is also lofty and with views, though as we have seen some at least of these must have been spoiled by 1933:

Pinner Hill stands at an altitude of some 400 feet above sea

152

level in the midst of glorious country surroundings, with extensive and beautiful views in all directions.

It really has everything, including being "dry above the average". Drier than Wembley? Drier than Malaga? Drier than the Sahara? I think we should be told.

It has unexcelled climatic conditions, being dry above the average, with indisputably healthy bracing air and a maximum of sunshine.

And there is more:

The shopping facilities are very good. There are excellent schools for boys and girls in the immediate district, and for recreation and sports one can find every form of indoor and outdoor amusement at hand There is the magnificent golf course at Pinner Hill. Both hunting and riding are also popular pastimes in this part. The Old Berkeley hunt often meets in the near neighbourhood.

Presumably the hunt must have run out of fields to ride across before too long, but

Pinner Hill may be termed a truly idyllic retreat as a permanent residence for the London business man.

The message is reinforced in the advertisement for the Country Gardens Estates development there:

Live and Play Golf at Pinner Hill

Surely the same thing?

This beautiful estate is considered to be the beauty spot of Middlesex.

It is over 400 feet above sea level and has delightful views in all directions.

The Pinner Hill Golf Course forms part of the Estate.

Several sites and houses are available, some overlooking the Golf Course. *[LAS]*

For once Briggs does not have much to say about the housing developments. He is more concerned about potential destruction of the village street, in this case unnecessarily.

> ... one could wish that such charming village streets as we still find at Pinner could be safeguarded, but if the lamentable change of the Edgware High Street from its former appearance to its present-day activity is to be a criterion, there is not much hope.
>
> Pinner contains a charming old inn near the church, a number of old shops and houses in the High Street, and the old building known as Dear's Farm in Bridge Street, about to be demolished ... . There are also many old farms around Pinner, including an interesting one with brick gables on the Uxbridge Road at Hatch End. *[MON]*

Holmes, on the other hand, laments the housing joining Pinner to Harrow but feels that the village street is in safe hands. In view of some of the municipal vandalism that occurred in the 1960s and 1970s, one might question whether "an era of conservation" had really arrived in the late 1930s, but it must have seemed so in comparison with the years immediately preceding.

> Pinner evidently intends, at no distant date, to become connected with Harrow by continuous links of brick and mortar. When the writer first saw the village street, the Metropolitan

Railway bridge which crosses it had been in position for only a few months, and the quiet thoroughfare was as drowsy, rural and unsophisticated as any to be found in remoter Wessex. Its picturesque character is still kept, and its many gabled old houses are unlikely to be demolished now that an era of conservation is with us. *[LC]*

Clunn's brief description of Pinner was no doubt accurate for 1935, but it is surprising that it was not changed for the post-war edition, by which time estates were no longer being "rapidly developed":

Now a thriving suburb of over 7,000 inhabitants ... The old village, situated on rising ground, forming the north-western side of Harrow Vale, consists principally of one broad main street sloping down to the Pin. It contains a mixture of old-fashioned shops and dwellings and well-built modern houses. ... Several large country houses are situated in this locality, but various residential estates are being rapidly developed, particularly in the direction of Harrow-on-the-Hill, two and three-quarter miles distant, which is now joined to Pinner by a continuous line of houses along the main London and Rickmansworth Road. *[TFL]*

Pevsner has a lot to say about Pinner in 1951, most of it good.

Still a compact little country town, though surrounded and overlaid by recent building in the "outer suburban" style. Up the High Street with several pretty half-timbered houses ... and Georgian brick houses one approaches the church. The vista is remarkably successful in an intimate way. On the left horse-chestnut trees screen off Church Farm, a long, low building of C18 and C17 date with weather-boarded barns behind. In the centre is the grey church tower and Sir Ernest George's Cocoa Tree Tavern [now Conservative Club; 1878] added to a plain

Georgian brick house. On the right the leafy Church Lane meanders away.

He also reveals that, at that date, a lot of the feeling of living in the countryside had been retained, at least in parts.

Further E Church Lane meets Nower Hill and Moss Lane. All this part of Pinner has still the character of well wooded countryside outside the town. Victorian and post-Victorian houses have large enough grounds not to disturb its character. Up Moss Lane to the N a cluster of farms is reached going back to Tudor days. Tudor Cottage is one of the most picturesque half-timbered farmhouses in the county. East End Farm has simple exposed timber framing. ... N of this hamlet suburban development interferes, and nothing of note is to be found until at the corner of Paines Lane Moss Cottage is reached with an irregular weather-boarded front and some Jacobean details inside. [BEM]

To see for myself, I arrive in Pinner High Street on another sunny afternoon, actually on the 5th of November, and it looks pretty much as it has done for centuries and as described above, except for the cars parked on either side. It would seem familiar to many who have never been here, if they were fans, as my family were, of the television comedy "May to December", which was set here. In the window of Corbett's Bookshop is a display of *Middlesex* by Michael Robbins, a paperback reprint of an excellent work, which is included under *Further Reading* near the beginning of this book. I pass the Queen's Head, again much as described in the books, and wonder who the gaffer is now. A long time ago it was nice man called Derek, who moved here from The Case is Altered in Eastcote. Walking in this direction up the High Street I feel there is something telling me that, despite appearances, I am not really in the centre of a small country

156

town, but it is hard to put my finger on it. Perhaps it is just that I know I am not! At the top of the hill the building which used to be Ye Cocoa Tree and then became the Conservative Club has a sign on it saying Howarths Homes, Elthorne Gate. I wonder what happened to the Conservatives; this is one place where you would not expect them to become extinct.

I walk past the church along Church Lane. It looks lovely in the sunshine and a sign outside says that it is open every day, a very nice change. There is a strange grave in the churchyard. According to the Guide for Visitors that I acquire later, "it was erected in 1809 by John Loudon who ... created the definitive Victorian villa of suburban London", a considerable claim to fame. "It was erected to mark the grave of his father, William, who for a long time held the lease of Wood Hall Farm". The story gets more interesting. "It consists of a tall pyramid, through the middle of which protrudes a stone coffin. William Loudon and his wife inherited some money under a will which stipulated that they should receive a certain sum so long as their bodies were above the ground. By burying his parents above the ground, a son sought to keep a bequest in the family". Who says that the suburbs are dull? The problem is that most of us for most of the time walk [or more likely drive] around without really looking at what surrounds us. However, in this case the Guide refers to the latter part of the story as a legend, so I check in *Pinner Through the Ages* by Walter Druett, from which it was obtained, and Druett says emphatically: "There is not a word of truth in the whole story ... but the legend is responsible for attracting visitors from all parts of the world". So, Pinner the Tourist Trap it is, but still not dull!

Church Cottage looks genuinely old, and Chestnut Cottage is pretty, with beautiful rowan berries on the wall, and there is a lovely old vicarage up a long drive. One vicar, perhaps, who has not been forced to move into a two-bedroom maisonette. Now I come to Pinner House, with a notice in the front from

Harrow Heritage Trust saying that it is possibly 17th century with façade completed in 1721. It was the home from 1788 to 1811 of Rev. Walter Williams, vicar of Pinner and Harrow, and his wife who was apparently a great-granddaughter of Charles the Second and Nell Gwynne. [Her name was Mary Beauclerc, for the benefit of trivia enthusiasts.] It doesn't say what the house is used for now, but judging by its modern extension and the old dears pottering around it looks like an old folks home.

It is very pretty along here, in what you might call a Victorian suburban way, though some of the houses are more recent. There is a big house called Mount View, which emphasises the fact that we are fairly high up [again, by Middlesex standards!] but I have not yet found a view. It seems that not much has changed round here since Pevsner's description and even a fairly modern detached house seems to fit in well. I arrive at a pleasant green triangle, with a variety of trees, retaining some leaves in a wonderful range of colours, and with a drinking fountain in the middle of it. The fountain is not working but its bears the inscription "Erected by the inhabitants of Pinner in grateful memory of the late William Arthur Tooke Esquire JP 1886, I was thirsty and you gave me drink". Piety and practicality, a very Victorian combination. I look down Nower Hill; not much to see though there are some nice Edwardian houses. Up here some of the houses are more modern but they all seem to be built in such a way that they fit in. I walk a short distance along Moss Lane and note that here there does seem to have been a lot of development since Pevsner's day, albeit mostly in keeping. I will take a quick look up Wakehams Hill in the hope of a view. Some of the houses here must get excellent ones and the sign for a new development offers "stunning views to the rear", but to start with I am disappointed. Then I see a fingerpost saying "Public Footpath no. 52" [very organised again!] "leading to George V Avenue", which

158

means that I can look through a gap in the trees down to Pinner Park. The prospect is interestingly mixed: the farm buildings are ahead of me in the middle of the fields, whilst over to my right is the Kodak building and various sorts of housing development. But beyond the farm it is mostly fields and trees, as it is to the left towards Pinner Hill and the golf course, with just a rather unsightly modern block of flats in the Woodridings/Hatch End direction. Before the coming of the Met, that is where the station was; a long way from Pinner. Overall I suppose the effect is more "country" than not, though there is a debate to be had on what the country-side really is. As I come away a couple of teenage schoolboys ask what I am doing and one of them at least seems moderately interested in my reply, so perhaps there's another potential customer.

I stop on my way back down Wakehams Hill. There is a large house at the bottom which obscures the view somewhat, but beyond it in the distance I can see the sun shining over Ruislip Woods, which makes me feel close to home. I suppose that I am really, but exploring on foot magnifies distances. Back at the green space where the fountain is, I take in again the mixture of trees, some natives like oaks, horse chestnuts and sycamores but some introduced, even exotic, "suburban" types, including what looks like a carob, the one that drops the sort of pods or husks that the Prodigal Son had to eat. There is a big house called Elmdene, I imagine about 100 years old and just the sort of place and name that you expect round here. There is also a little cottage here that I did not notice on the way up and which looks genuinely old, at least in parts, but I cannot see a name on the gate.

It is interesting to see the church from this direction, rather than in the context of the High Street. It does look like a, slightly grand, country church and the High Street itself seems more rural from this angle. I now see a notice on the wall of the building next to the church saying "Designed by Ernest

George and Peto, built for Judge William Barber of Barrow-point House as a temperance tavern in 1878. Its tea garden attracted visitors from London. It flourished until the late 1920s as Ye Cocoa Tree then it became the local Conservative Club until the 1960s". Church Farm looks very distinguished, half-timbered, partly pebbledashed and I cannot really add anything to Pevsner. Walking down the High Street I am impressed by how the character has been preserved despite the adaptation of the buildings to modern usage, including David Charles Estate Agent and Pizza Express. The actual bridge in Bridge Street is now a modern metal affair and a quick look shows that the Pinn is rather uninteresting here, confined in a concrete channel.

When I get back to the car park I find that an overstay of seven minutes [due to peeping in to both the church and the bookshop] has been rewarded with a fine of £40. As it was crawling with wardens when I arrived, and there is no sign now of the little storm trooper who did for me, I can only assume that they lurk underground and pop up as soon as your back is turned. Pretty Pinner may be, but it does not seem to welcome visitors, or not ones that come by car anyway.

Trying to put this harrowing experience behind me, I drive along Moss Lane, which, as I have already remarked, seems to have undergone a lot of development since the days of Pevsner. It is still attractive but there are a number of modern houses among the trees. The Tudor Cottage is still here and a sign saying "Visitors only to East End House, East End Farm ... private road, no parking", so at least one farm is still here [farmhouse at any rate]. The road twists and turns more as I go along, like the country lane it was, albeit now lined with large detached houses behind their high hedges. When I come out at Paines Lane I find Moss Cottage on the corner. To complete my attempted recovery from the parking fine I drive along George V Avenue through Pinner Park Farm and do

160

get a little taste of the country, though the wire mesh fences are rather ugly.

I set out again the following morning, hoping that the sun is going to put in an appearance and keen to avoid the little Hitlers of central Pinner, because there are other areas that I want to see. I stop first on Pinner Hill; lovely trees along the side and millionaires' row type of houses. This really is Posh Pinner, as advertised in *London and Suburbs*. I am going to be really daring and go down a road that says "Private Road, Residents and Pinner Hill Golf Club Only. Unauthorised plebeian vehicles will be removed" [all right, I have added one word]. This is Park View Road and it gets posher and posher, though a perfectionist might suggest that the houses are a little close together and some turn out to be in rather better taste than others. The golf clubhouse is a rather gloomy Victorian building. At the end of the road there is an inviting, leaf-strewn path through the trees, leading to the open hill. A good approximation to countryside. Up here near the county border is where the better-heeled citizens live, though it becomes increasingly the case as I go along that some of the houses speak more of money than of good taste. As I round a corner I get something of a view, though it is rather misty today. I like what I can see, though as ever it is fair to say that the fact that building stopped here makes the houses that were put up all the more desirable. As I come out of the little estate past the "Private" notices I get a "What's an oik like you doing here?" look from a mutton-dressed-as-lamb lady, with an unnaturally brown face and dyed blonde hair. A glance at the map later shows that none of the roads I have been on [except the one called Pinner Hill] actually exist. If you have enough money you can apparently persuade A to Z to keep your territory uncharted!

I stop next to a rather strange structure with a sign saying "Pinner Hill Farm, The Folly, The High Barn" with a little farmyard and then turn into Albury Drive, where I have been

161

told that the houses were built as Artisans' Dwellings. To start with, the houses look like post-WW2 council, of the better sort but nothing special, but then I come to what must have been the "artisans'" houses, nice and cottagey like the less grand ones in Hampstead Garden Suburb. Looking straight down the road I can see Harrow Weald Common and the whole place has a pleasant feel to it, with the houses on the left built right up to the hill. They were obviously designed for humbler folk than those on millionaires' row, but even humble folk get nice surroundings here. [Of course, the current residents may not be very humble anyway!] Continuing en route to the Woodhall Estate, there are lovely trees, quite mature, and the first houses are modest [but probably not cheap] semis in interesting styles and showing their pre-WW1 origins. I turn left along Woodhall Gate where the houses are of similar vintage but grander, and in some cases detached. There is a spot that is beautifully green here and not too tended, a residual patch of the Hill as it was.

I go a short distance east along the Uxbridge Road to look at Woodridings, passing a nostalgic maroon British Railways sign pointing to Hatch End Station. I enter Wellington Road, Woodridings. The first houses I see are Victorian, followed by Edwardian-looking ones, some semis but on a big scale and one or two in the Arts and Crafts style. Woodridings Avenue is also very nice, with a little twitten through to Pinner Park. It is really quite quiet here, with even the sound of the cars on George V Avenue rather muffled in the distance, and the birdsong predominates. There is some pasture land ahead of me with cows grazing in front of the farm. What I see depends on where I look; there is a lot of farmland as a reminder of the Middlesex countryside that was, but in the distance I can also see the Kodak chimneys. Back on Woodridings Avenue it still seems very quiet except for the birds. The houses appear to be a hundred or so years old and are of a mixture of sizes but good looking with beautiful trees in front of them and, on the south side, with the park behind them. At the end are some allotments and a twitten through to the Hatch End shopping area, and somewhere over there I get a glimpse of the square block I saw from the hill and which stands out from the semis that surround it and seem more in keeping with the semi-rural surroundings.

I now drive on to take a look at Royston Park, passing through Hatch End's commonplace-looking suburban shopping street, though it has to be said that it is a glorious tribute to town planning compared with its equivalent in Eastcote. I turn left up The Avenue, which consists initially of small blocks of flats, but is a nice wide road with beautiful horse chestnut trees. I decide to go to the end, partly to find out if I can see where the railway cuts through Grim's Dyke, but all I find is a rather nondescript piece of open space with a wire mesh fence and a notice saying "Caution, Demolition Work in Progress" and, more mysteriously, "Attention. Sensitive Site. No shouting. Do not leave litter. Switch off vehicles. Minimise reversing. Please take extra care". Underneath it says "Railtrack West Coast Modernisation". Well, if it is railway land I suppose it explains why it looks scruffy, and I am not able to see where the line goes through Grim's Dyke. But why am I forbidden to shout? It is an incomprehensible edict that makes me want to bellow at the top of my voice but I restrain myself. In any case, I understand that Failtrack has been replaced now by Notwork Rail. Away from the railway this estate is very pleasant, as is Pinner in general. Royston Park Road is again wide and tree-lined but in this case with very substantial and pleasant houses on it. The one that I stop in front of has a notice on the gate saying "Hatch End Horticultural Society presents a talk on The Fruit in the Garden, by Gerry Edwards". This is suburbia at its best! In Pinner everything is nice. Except the traffic wardens, who are offensively sneaky. Indeed, every prospect pleases and only man [one anyway] is vile.

It now comes home to me that, as I have mentioned earlier, many of the areas that I have looked at are some way from the Met line and that I have not yet done full justice to Metro-land Pinner. To do so I will have to return to the centre, but take care not to park for more than a millisecond. I particularly want to see the Grange Estate, the one with the artistic houses. Also the Cecil Park Estate and Cannon Croft. I emerge at more open space on Oxhey Lane, just across from Grim's Dyke, or Grim's Ditch as it is shown on my map. I decide to take a look. There is a pleasant golf course but with a huge ugly telecoms mast behind it. It is a real problem these days getting away from such things, and now Prescott wants to put up hulking wind farms everywhere as well. I can just see the ditch running up the golf course. The road opposite is Old Redding, which runs to W.S. Gilbert's old house and one of the [at least] three pubs round here called The Case is Altered. Getting back into the car I turn right into Oxhey Lane, away from Oxhey itself, the south part of which I believe was the location for *Tropic of Ruislip*. Sounds interesting; perhaps I should go there some day! I emerge on the Uxbridge Road opposite the old prefab-style council houses, which perhaps break the rule that all housing round here of whatever level is nice, but they are not without interest and I am pleased that they survive. The first girl I ever walked home was a postman's daughter called Simone, and she lived in a house like that. Further along there are some real Metro-land houses, nice Tudorbethan semis, just before I cross back over the railway line.

Arriving at the Grange Estate I go into Grange Gardens, where the houses are upmarket Metro-land, some semis but large, and flowering cherries along the way. It is all very nice indeed [except for the yellow lines in front of the houses] and seems to show Metropolitan Railway Country Estates Ltd at their very best. But Artistic? Now to the other side of the tracks, into Cecil Park. A variety of houses here, some quite

164

large, but without quite such an upmarket feel to it as on the Grange. The road is quite wide but there are fewer trees and some of the front gardens are concreted over. Overall, not quite as "Pinner", but still Metro-land. A quick look down Cannon Lane, which I suppose is on the Cannon Croft Estate; slightly humbler dwellings with semis and small terraces, but pleasant enough. If I follow this it looks as if it will take me to good old Rayners Lane and as I go along it remains pleasant but tends more towards endless suburban monotony. As I have said before, between Rayners Lane and Eastcote the monotonous side of Metro-land kicks in. Nothing wrong with it, but too much of it. Pinner is better, for those with the money.

Further reading

Pinner Through The Ages Walter W. Druett, The Hillingdon Press, 3rd edition, 1965

Panorama of Pinner Village E.J.S. Gadsden [ed.], Panorama of Pinner Publishing Committee, 1969

Harrow before your time Pinner and Hatch End W.E.A. Local History Group, 1972

Harrow walkabout Elizabeth Cooper, Pinner and Hatch End W.E.A., 1973

The Countryside Lies Sleeping Alan W. Ball, The Riverhill Press, 1981

Pinner, A Pictorial History Patricia A. Clarke, Phillimore, 1994

Afterword

In the Foreword I quoted the view of Oliver Green that, by the late 1930s, development had " ... transformed many districts from open countryside to drab and monotonous suburban sprawl. The notion of Metro-land as a rural Arcadia no longer matched the suburban reality of Wembley Park or Rayners Lane, although the outer areas beyond Rickmansworth still retained their country character". In the course of writing this book I have tramped the mean streets of six Middlesex "villages" with my little Dictaphone, observing and recording their current appearance and comparing my impressions with the evolving historic picture presented by the contemporary accounts, and with Green's downbeat assessment. The aim in this final section is to summarise what I have learnt, crystallise my current feelings about the Middlesex section of Metro-land as it is today and see if any lessons can be identified relevant to the current planning debate. My views and feelings are summarised below, and I trust that not *all* of them will be seen as statements of the blinding obvious.

Metro-land was an inherently contradictory concept

As the homes were built in the countryside, that countryside disappeared. Where any of it remains, the retrospective thanks are due to not to the Met and its agents, or to other developers, but to local authorities or, in the case of Harrow, a school. Left to themselves, developers will develop, and justify their activities and the accompanying profits on the basis that they are meeting a need. Indeed, at one level they must be, or the houses would not sell. None of this of course represents original thought and similar points were made in some of the texts quoted. But it remains relevant. I saw the following advertisement in *The Times* of 3rd October 2003: "The Paddocks, Silver Street, Goff's Oak, Hertfordshire. Surrounded by a patchwork of fields, in peaceful countryside, The Paddocks is a rural idyll. The gated five acre site is the tranquil, secluded location for some of Hertfordshire's most desirable executive family homes. Prices £395,000–£770,500." The copy could have come from the pages of *Metro-land* the publication, or is a direct descendant. Words and phrases like "desirable", "executive" and "gated site" each convey a clear meaning, particularly when linked to "rural idyll" and "tranquil, secluded location". Presumably the idyll is less rural, and the location less tranquil and secluded, than before the homes were developed. As a corollary ...

Houses become most desirable where the building stops

My own house carries a price premium because it faces farmland. The first people to protest about a new development are often those who live in houses built on an adjacent field a few years earlier. Some of the most desirable roads that I have seen on my Metro-land travels have been those next to where the building stopped, for whatever reason. When I was in areas where the building did not stop until all the fields had disappeared, I sometimes wondered to what extent the early arrivals were told about the future plans for development that would destroy their country views. Perhaps they did not mind, being mainly attracted to a pleasant house with all mod cons at a price that they could afford, which just happened to be close to the village of [say] Ruislip. In truth ...

Not everyone wants to live in the countryside

Or indeed in the suburbs. Many of the traditionally most expensive parts of London, such as Belgravia, are close to the centre, and these have been joined in the last thirty years by the gentrification of areas such as Islington and Battersea and, more recently, the redevelopment of Docklands for the terminally hip. Furthermore ...

What is the countryside anyway?

Metro-land the publication always stressed the fact that housing development was [or would be] accompanied by the provision of amenities such as new roads, shopping parades, tennis courts and cinemas. In most cases house buyers did not intend to keep chickens, nor did they envisage themselves trudging along muddy lanes to get to a village shop. They were seeking an improved lifestyle, which included the perceived health benefits of moving away from the inner city, but it was not a rural one. Today, the question takes on a deeper meaning. For fifty plus years from the beginning of WW2, the countryside was primarily viewed as being for food production, as efficiently [intensively] as possible, with recreational or environmental benefits very much secondary. Now food production in the UK is increasingly uneconomic, and the countryside is viewed as being either about those previously subsidiary purposes or, in some official eyes, for *building on*. This is not an academic debate. In Ickenham, a part of Middlesex Metro-land that has retained some genuine agriculture, the farmer across the road has had to get out of dairying and the future of the land is in doubt. It is "inalienable" Green Belt, but he cannot make a living farming it conventionally, and his plans for limited beef production coupled with a range of commercial and environmental projects [for the latter of which he has the support of the Herts and Middlesex Wildlife Trust], are not at time of writing being viewed favourably by the pen pushers of the "London" Borough of Hillingdon. If the land becomes an eyesore, there

169

are no prizes for guessing what will come next. But returning to the more general point, all of the "villages" that I have covered have at least parts that are close to real open space, apart from municipal parks, and could be said to fulfil the Metro-land promise. Even in Wembley, the start of Metro-land and where parts seem degraded beyond recall, the fortunate dwellers on the Barn Hill Estate have the remaining undeveloped part of the hill itself and the adjoining Fryent Country Park. Away from Barn Hill, there are areas even of Wembley that may not have a rural outlook, but where if you like this sort of suburbia, this is the sort of suburbia you will like. It must be borne in mind, however, that ...

Money counts

I do not mean by this that richer people have better taste than poorer people, as a walk down either of Ickenham's million-aires' rows will demonstrate, at least in my humble opinion. However, it is true in general that money can buy space and that the more expensive houses tend to be built on the more interesting land. This is illustrated not only by Barn Hill but also in, for instance, Ruislip, where the "better" areas are to the north, where the land is hillier and the forest and farmland closer. As we have seen, on the broad plain to the south the semis individually are fine, but their serried rows seem to stretch for ever.

And so does lack of money

Some of our fellow citizens have a rabid hatred for their surroundings, which unfortunately are ours too. If they want to live like pigs in their own sties that is their right, but when they pollute public places it is another matter. From crisp packets and McDonald's wrappings to fly tipping and

170

abandoned cars, their moronic activities scar the fair[ish] face of Metro-land, particularly the streams, woodlands and other relics of the former countryside. The authorities nationally or locally sometimes talk a good game but do little in practice to curb these obnoxious scum, usually blaming a lack of money, though it might be argued that it is sometimes more a case of how they choose to spend the large wads of cash that they take from us. Similarly, they are reluctant to clear up mess once it has been created. It takes so little to make or mar so much. But despite everything ...

Metro-land is marvellous

At least a great deal of it is! For the purposes of this book I have ignored "the outer areas beyond Rickmansworth" in leafy, expensive Bucks and Herts. But even in despised, forgotten, built-over Middlesex I have visited or revisited many places of considerable, if largely unpretentious, beauty and many others that provide a pleasant environment to live in, surely the underlying promise of Metro-land's promoters. Even areas that appear less promising at first sight may, as in the case of Rayners Lane, be much more attractive away from the main roads and the run down, architecturally challenged, shopping parades. My first ten years in a Wembley semi seem to have left me a Metro-land man, with a love of my own "parcel of English soil in which to build home and strike root". Though it has to be said that the suburban pride of territorial possession can get out of hand. *The Times* of 11th November 2003 carried a story that started as follows. "A row between two neighbours over a six-inch strip of land ... left them with costs of almost £150,000. Tempers flared in the suburb of Kenton, Middlesex when Marie Dunne tried to have a fence moved a few feet to accommodate an extension to her home ...".

171

What is the future for Metro-land?

Some of the challenges have already been mentioned, such as the future of remaining farmland, like that surrounding most of Ickenham and stretching to Harefield. The constant and growing traffic menace has been a recurring theme in this book and seems to have no obvious answers, outside the scheming brain of Red Ken. The developers of Metro-land could hardly have foreseen these problems, or those stemming from changes in leisure and shopping patterns. Where they may have been more culpable is in some of their building standards. According to a worrying article by Jeff Howell, in the *Sunday Telegraph* of 11th January 2004, "Shoddy standards lie behind suburbia's slide". In the piece he compares the building standards and design of 1930s semis unfavourably with those of their Victorian and Edwardian predecessors: "While they had a core of solid brickwork, they also had front bays and mock-Tudor gables built from expanded metal lathing, tacked on to a light timber framework and plastered or pebble dashed over. As the semis reach their three-score-years-and ten, some of this stuff is simply falling to bits". He also mentions problems with poorly maintained windows, resulting in a hotchpotch of unsuitable PVC replace-ments, and the concreting over of front gardens for car parking. I have been very aware of the latter two of these problems, if not the first, on my perambulations. The solution? "What is needed. of course, is investment – grants and refurbishment incentives – to adapt the semis to modern standards, and restore them to their former glories. The alter-native is to see them bulldozed, and replaced with more modern housing, which will have an even shorter life expec-tancy". Speaking from the heart, as one "born and brought up in a 1930s semi", he says that such a result would be unthinkable. However, in a world where the authorities cannot or will not police the streets or even pick up rubbish, the prospect of these grants and incentives seems a little remote. In any case, money is not the only issue. The high value of many of these homes may encourage their owners to invest their own money in maintenance and improvement, but the results may not be in keeping with the original style, or indeed with basic good taste. We will have to hope that the situation is not *quite* as bad as Howell suggests!

Does the Metro-land experience have lessons for elsewhere?

Perhaps only the obvious ones. If Elysium is even partly lost, that part can never be regained. The nicest areas of Middlesex now are those with the most space, either for individual houses or for communities, but to use this as a blueprint would, apart from the prohibitive cost, lead to suburbanisation of even more of the precious English countryside that remains. Part of the solution must lie in a more serious commitment to "brownfield" development than currently seems the case, and there is plenty of scope, even in Middlesex. Planning is clearly important, and played a role in particular in the way that Ruislip developed, but post-war planning also produced tower block estates and urban ring roads so it is not a panacea. The big issue is the demand. It fuelled the growth of Metro-land and is there now, as reflected in the continuing [as at January 2004] rise in house prices, despite many forecasts to the contrary. Although the Government appears to be incapable of producing accurate figures for anything, there is no doubt that the demand is fuelled in part by a rise in the population. But the prospect of real action to curb further immigration, much of it illegal, is remote, with some ministers apparently wanting to increase it, in order to provide sweated labour for the jobs the natives do not want. In any case, the even more serious problem is the increase in the number of households due to marriage breakdowns. Even

I would be hard put to blame this entirely on the Government, but its conversion to the "family friendly" policies so beloved of *Telegraph* and *Mail* readers seems unlikely.

In conclusion

As I approach the end of this small-scale odyssey, my feelings about the Middlesex part of Metro-land are as ambivalent as, I believe, were those of Betjeman. I would have loved to see Middlesex as a rural county and would have hated to watch as it was built up, but quite like much [not all] of how it looks today. My "walks with a purpose" have shown me how much of interest that I miss when driving around in the normal course of things. I have seen the site of "the first recorded motor accident in Great Britain involving the death of the driver" and puzzled at the Railtrack sign in Pinner, saying "Sensitive site. No shouting". I have seen where the houses invaded the fields and where the fields and open spaces still sit alongside the houses. I have enjoyed revisiting my "primary sources" and hope that I may have encouraged a few others to seek out these works in libraries, secondhand bookshops and book fairs. I wish that I could have met some of the authors, in particular Gordon Maxwell. Could his conversation be as stimulating and lively as his prose? He loved Middlesex and was rightly concerned about its development, but I trust he would agree with me that this particular Elysium has not been entirely lost.

LIVE IN METRO-LAND!

Index

175

176

Greenhill, Harrow *107, 111, 112,*
    117, 122, 128, 135
Green Man, Wembley *19, 28, 36*
Greenway, The, Ickenham *52*
Grim[m]'s Dyke/Ditch, Harrow/
    Pinner *136, 146, 163, 164*
Grosvenor Vale, Ruislip *82*
Grove Hill, Harrrow *133*
Grove Hill Road, Harrow *134*
Grove, The, Ickenham *48*
Guildford *132*
Gwynne, Nell *158*

Hailsham, Lord *49*
Hamilton, Lady *145*
Hampstead *108, 130*
Hampstead Garden Suburb *162*
Hanger Lane *10*
Harefield *41, 65, 172*
Harefield Place *41*
Harrow **Ch 5**, *9, 13, 20, 22, 44, 45,
    55, 58, 141, 143, 149, 150, 152,
    154, 158, 167*
Harrow Garden Village/Estate *118,
    119, 120, 121, 122, 124, 137, 138*
Harrow Golf Club *116*
Harrow Heritage Trust *158*
Harrow Hill/Harrow-on-the-Hill *5,
    19, 32, 35, 39, 105, 106, 107,
    109, 110, 111, 113, 114, 115,
    116, 117, 122, 125, 127, 129,
    130, 131, 132, 133, 134, 135,
    138, 155*
Harrow Museum and Heritage
    Centre *129*
Harrow-on-the-Hill [Met] Station
    112, 123
Harrow Park *108, 112, 130*
Harrow Recreation Grounds *114*
Harrow Road, Wembley *22, 31, 32*
Harrow School *105, 106, 111, 113,
    114, 115, 116, 125, 127, 131,
    132, 133, 134, 135, 167*
Harrow [and Wealdstone] Station
    107, 111, 112

Harrow Urban District Council *132*
Harrow Weald *35, 107, 112, 113,
    115, 128, 133, 143,* 162
Harrow Weald Common *112, 136,
    162*
Haste Hill, Ruislip *62, 71, 91*
Hatch End *128, 141, 142, 143, 145,
    146, 149, 150, 154, 159, 163*
Hatch End Horticultural Society *163*
[Pinner and] Hatch End Station *142,
    145, 146, 159, 162*
Hawthorn Way, Eastcote *100*
Hawtrey Drive, Ruislip *81*
Hawtrey family *81, 88*
hay/hayfields/grass *6, 11, 34, 41, 46,
    57, 107, 111*
Haydon Hall, Eastcote *88, 90, 91,
    94, 95, 98*
Haydon Lodge, Eastcote *95*
Hayes *55, 110*
Haymills Ltd. [builders] *24, 25, 36*
Headingley *102*
Headstone Estate, Harrow *113, 135,
    136*
Headstone Lane, Harrow *129*
Headstone Manor/Moat Farm,
    Harrow *109, 112, 113, 115, 119,
    120, 122, 123, 128, 129, 136,
    143*
health *22, 25, 43, 60, 66, 68, 69, 113,
    114, 124, 125, 153, 169*
Heath [builders] *46*
Hemmings, David *138*
Hendon *20*
Hendon Rural District Council *120,
    149, 152*
Henry VI *74*
Herga House, Harrow *130*
Hermitage, The *109*
Herts *12, 171*
Herts and Middlesex Wildlife Trust
    169
Heston *111*
Hewlett, Geoffrey *34, 35*
Highgate *6, 108, 130*

178

179

London and North-Western Railway *112, 126, 141, 142, 143, 145*

London Encyclopaedia, The 87

London Midland and Scottish Railway *126*

London's Metropolitan Railway 12

London Stock Exchange *37*

London's Underground Suburbs 10

Long Lane, Ickenham *49, 51*

Long Lane Farm, Ickenham *50*

Loudon, John *157*

Loudon, William *157*

Lyon Farm, Wembley *29*

McDonald's *78, 95, 99, 170*

Malaga *153*

Manor Farm, Ruislip *59, 73, 74, 75, 76*

Manor Farm Estate, Ruislip *65, 66*

Manor House/Farm, Ickenham *50*

Manor Way, Ruislip *80*

marriage breakdown *173*

Marylebone Station *52*

Mary Queen of Scots *28*

"May to December" [sitcom] *156*

Memorials of Old Middlesex 10

Metro-land [publication] *12, 13, 37, 49, 69, 126, 137, 168, 169*

Metro-land as a concept *12, 13, 19, 23, 26, 27, 34, 37, 46, 70, 75, 77, 78, 79, 80, 81, 85, 117, 125, 126, 129, 130, 133, 135, 136, 149, 151, 164, 165, 167, 168, 169, 170, 171, 172, 173, 174*

Metropolitan Railway/Line *9, 12, 21, 28, 33, 42, 50, 52, 59, 60, 62, 63, 66, 70, 71, 89, 91, 96, 114, 115, 118, 119, 120, 126, 138, 142, 143, 146, 147, 148, 149, 150, 151, 154, 159, 164, 167*

Metropolitan Railway Country Estates Ltd. *12, 43, 66, 164*

Metropolitan Railway Surplus Lands Committee *120, 149*

Metropolitan Tower Construction Company Ltd. *21*

Midcroft Way, Ruislip *80*

Middlesex *5, 9, 10, 11, 12, 14, 16, 19, 45, 55, 56, 57, 62, 63, 70, 72, 88, 89, 91, 96, 109, 110, 111, 128, 131, 136, 153, 158, 162, 167, 169, 171, 173, 174*

Middlesex County Council *152*

Mill Farm, Ruislip *73*

Mill Hill *113*

Mills and Co. [builders] *29*

Missouri Court, Eastcote *97*

Mr Standfast 27

Moderne style *81, 137*

Money *37, 61, 78, 80, 101, 106, 111, 112, 125, 129, 130, 148, 161, 165, 170, 171, 173*

Morford Close, Eastcote *100*

Morford Way, Eastcote *100*

Moss Cottage, Pinner *156, 160*

Moss Lane, Pinner *156, 158, 160*

motor accident [first recorded] *133, 174*

Mount Stewart Avenue, Harrow *138*

Mount View, Pinner *158*

Myrtle Avenue, Ruislip/Eastcote *82*

Nash, T.F. [builders] *93*

Neasden *10*

Nelson, Lord *145*

Newlands, Harrow *131*

Nicholson, Sir William *97*

North Circular Road *31*

North Harrow/Station *114, 116, 118, 119, 124, 125, 128, 131, 133, 135, 136, 137, 149*

Northolt *5, 83, 91, 102, 108, 119*

Northolt Aerodrome/Airport *70, 73, 74, 83*

Northolt Junction/South Ruislip Station *71*

Northolt Park *69*

North View, Eastcote *100*

Northwick Estate, Harrow *116, 138*

182